NAVIGATING
ROCKY TERRAIN

NAVIGATING ROCKY TERRAIN

Caves, Karsts, and the Soul of Unseen Spaces

LAURIE ROATH FRAZIER

MAVERICK BOOKS / TRINITY UNIVERSITY PRESS
San Antonio

Maverick Books, an imprint of Trinity University Press
San Antonio, Texas 78212

Book design by BookMatters, Berkeley
Cover design by Anne Richmond Boston

978-1-59534-288-1 paperback
978-1-59534-289-8 ebook

Names of some individuals in this book have been changed out of respect
for privacy.

Trinity University Press strives to produce its books using methods and
materials in an environmentally sensitive manner. We favor working
with manufacturers that practice sustainable management of all natural
resources, produce paper using recycled stock, and manage forests with
the best possible practices for people, biodiversity, and sustainability.
The press is a member of the Green Press Initiative, a nonprofit program
dedicated to supporting publishers in their efforts to reduce their impacts
on endangered forests, climate change, and forest-dependent communities.

The paper used in this publication meets the minimum requirements of the
American National Standard for Information Sciences—Permanence of
Paper for Printed Library Materials, ANSI 39.48-1992.

CIP data on file at the Library of Congress

28 27 26 25 24 | 5 4 3 2 1

CONTENTS

INTRODUCTION

At first, I thought I was writing a science story, a story about karst ecology. As a writer and biologist, I am drawn to places that lie hidden in plain sight and to things that happen all around us, unseen. Usually this leads me to small finds, like nests or cocoons, but this time was different. In the Texas Hill Country where I live, an enormous crevice, a gorge, formed following a flood. As floodwaters carved through the bedrock and then receded, hidden subterranean layers were exposed at the surface.

The gorge tugged at my imagination, held me in place, and before long, cracks and holes became my obsession: where did they lead and what kinds of plants and animals lived there? I set off on a journey to learn more about the science of what happens beneath the surface.

Early on, the story took an unexpected turn. As I explored karst terrain, I felt a connection to the landscape, as if the changes and losses—the cracks and holes—in my own life were becoming more visible at the surface. They, too, required exploration and understanding. I started mapping the back-and-forth between surface and subterranean ecosystems and between my own inner and outer worlds.

As I traveled through the Hill Country spending time with rivers, sinkholes, springs, and caves, landforms that character-ize karst landscapes, I carried these questions with me as guides:

What is life like in cracked and shattered places? How do people and places—plants, animals, and the land—heal following a disturbance? How does life flourish in the shadow of uncertainty?

My essays delved deeper and evolved into much more than a science story. They represented a searching: a desire to find healing, hope, and home during a tumultuous time in my life. As I struggled, I recognized the struggles of a landscape enduring ongoing environmental upheaval, and as I got to know the karst places and the people working to protect them, both stories—the scientific and the personal—merged on a path toward restoration.

PART ONE

SHIFTING

It was Independence Day, 2002. Although I was miles from Central Texas, I imagine that day. Except for the rhythm of sheets of rain that pounded the earth with extraordinary force, silence pervaded the landscape. The whistles and trills of mockingbirds, the constant chatter of scissor-tailed flycatchers, the whoosh of vultures' wings as they swooped down to perch on leafless branches—the sounds of place—ceased abruptly, as if a warning had been cast through the air: *take shelter.*

One week earlier, on June 29, a low-pressure storm had stalled over Central Texas. The Army Corps of Engineers closed the parks and marinas surrounding Canyon Lake on July 3. Over the holiday weekend, the local government also ordered the evacuation of homes, campgrounds, and resorts, forcing more than one thousand residents and tourists from the immediate area. Downriver, more evacuations would follow. Soon a restless energy had spread as both the human and nonhuman community awaited the inevitable.

Three feet of rain, more than typically falls in one year, saturated the land. The resulting mega flood began swallowing roads and bridges, and where houses stood, only rooftops peeked above the rising water. In less than a week, Canyon Lake reservoir had filled to nearly one and a half times the normal level. Residents feared the earthen dam would burst.

Around 3 p.m. on July 4, a seven-foot wall of water crashed over the dam's emergency spillway, tearing through the river valley below. For six weeks, the stormwaters poured over the banks of the Guadalupe River and its tributaries, scattering debris—trees, cattle, boulders, bridges, cars, and homes—as far as the Gulf Coast, almost two hundred miles away. Thirty-four counties were declared federal disaster areas. Nearly fifty thousand homes and businesses were damaged or destroyed. Nine people lost their lives.

And what the water left behind shocked everyone: a gorge, one mile long and fifty feet deep, exposing the earth's inner layers like a gaping wound.

Scientists use the phrase "ecological shift" to describe the events that follow a catastrophic disturbance like this one. The basic structure and function of the preexisting ecosystem disappears, while the land and its inhabitants struggle to adapt to new circumstances, to evolve.

My mother delivered her legendary lemon meringue pie to the Christmas table for the last time in 2009. She was sixty-eight years old. Earlier that day in the kitchen, she flittered back and forth between the counter, the pantry, and the sink. She wrung her hands and fiddled with her wedding ring. She stared at the recipe, searched for ingredients in the pantry, and returned empty-handed again and again. In our family, old recipes, like tattered maps, tell stories of time and place and people—most are committed to memory.

As she worked, the muscles in my mother's face tensed, her body stiffened. She refused my help with a wave of her hand. It was well past my children's bedtime when she finally placed the pie before us, the meringue floating like broken icebergs adrift in a pale-yellow sea. I jumped up from my chair, switched out bowls for plates, and the meal continued as if nothing unusual had happened.

*   *   *

On a mild February morning, almost seventeen years after the mega flood, I set out to hike the aftermath, Canyon Lake Gorge, fifty miles north of San Antonio and nine miles northwest of my house. A guide, two docents, and a family from Nebraska complete the tour group. According to the geological map, some of the spots we will visit include Upper Pond, the Waterfalls, the Pit, the Lagoon, and Lower Pond.

After a few brief introductions, we board a shuttle bus and head to the site. Alongside the shuttle, the dam towers over us: a sheer earthen wall, nearly as tall as the Statue of Liberty and more than a mile long, covered in neatly mown grass. In 1958 the U.S. Army Corps of Engineers constructed the dam and its reservoir, Canyon Lake, to control flooding in the Guadalupe River valley and to conserve water. Today the reservoir serves as a source of drinking water, and the dam produces hydroelectric power. On Friday afternoons, tourists and locals flock to the lake, hauling boats, Jet Skis, wakeboards, and tubes. The project, an engineering feat, held up well until the massive flood of 2002—the first and only time the reservoir flooded the emergency spillway, which had been created to reduce water pressure on the dam.

Exiting the shuttle, we search on foot for the gorge that lies hidden beyond dense stands of huisache and Ashe juniper trees. The terrain changes abruptly. From the ledge, the gaping crack in the earth below is as deep as a five-story building is tall. It is vast and empty, a desert of broken rock, the bare bones of a river that winds downhill for more than a mile. The wind whips through the sunken landscape as if we are standing beside a wind tunnel. Down a series of stone steps laid by volunteers, we enter the gorge.

The floodwaters carved through the limestone bedrock, revealing layers of geological information dating back 100 million years. Under normal conditions, a gorge like this would take millions of years to form, similar to the Grand Canyon, but this one formed in just three days. By comparing photographs of the landscape before and after, scientists gain a unique opportunity from the gorge to learn about the past from the present.

My eyes absorb the colors—charcoal, cream, and a hundred subtle shades of brown—running like rivulets along the rock walls. While newly exposed Cretaceous limestone is white, a result of the layering of shells from ancient marine organisms, this sedimentary rock has changed over time. On the surface of the rock, the buildup of impurities such as sand, clay, and iron oxide, and living organisms, like lichen, cause color changes and provide geographic information about the stones' origins. I trace the waves of color with my fingertips; the crumbling surface is rough and cool.

Starting our descent, the contrast between the gorge and what lies on either side is striking: before and after, green and brown, trees and rock. A sense of isolation comes with the knowledge that life—soil, oak trees, armadillos, wild turkeys, roadrunners, and deer—was swept away so quickly.

We step down onto large flat sheets of rock scattered with boulders. It is a shattered and disconnected landscape, like a giant puzzle whose pieces have fallen on the floor and no longer fit together. Walking along what resembles a dry riverbed, we see spindly, neon-orange flags poking out from between rocks to encourage us to stay on the "path." We are watchful of our footing and help each other maneuver over the erratic obstacle course made of loose stone. If I were alone, it would be easy to become disoriented and stray off the trail, unnoticed.

My mother traveled from Virginia to Texas in spring 2013 for the birth of my third son, to help just as she had done before. The day after she arrived, we headed straight to her favorite Mexican restaurant. Without picking up the menu, she asked me to order for her. During our conversation, I sensed the invisible fog that masked my mother's larger-than-life personality and sharp wit. She preferred to listen now, to settle into the background.

My contractions started as we savored our last few bites of *enchiladas verdes*, and after speaking with a nurse on the phone, we returned home to pack my bag for the hospital stay. I lay in bed, as directed, and told my mother where to find my clothes. She struggled to follow directions; left, right, up, and down had become complicated concepts. As a test, I asked her to drive us to the hospital, to see if she would be able to take my older sons home later that night. (My husband and I had hoped to spend the first night together with our new baby.) Although she should have been familiar with the route, she wasn't. She drove twenty miles an hour down the four-lane highway. In that moment, life shifted; for the first time, my mother needed me more than I needed her.

We take a short rest about halfway down the Canyon Gorge Trail. I break away from the group and sit on a bench near a waterfall. Emerald green water gushing out of a fracture in the limestone surprises me. This is a place that encourages silent contemplation, where everything bubbles just beneath the surface. Although my thoughts are scattered, the land waits patiently, ready to engage in conversation.

Before returning to the trail, I rummage through my backpack. I hang my camera around my neck, slip my hand lens around my wrist, and cram my notebook under my arm. My awkward appearance doesn't deter me from my newfound mission: the sudden urge to document the existence of living things. Maybe it has something to do with the emptiness—the feeling of solitude—that lurks in the gorge. Maybe it is the mysterious need to connect to this place that rises inexplicably from within. I strain my eyes, seeking the smallest traces of life.

Close to the ground, life becomes visible again, things with familiar names: the fluffy seed heads of brushy bluestem, a brave

dung beetle teetering across the rocks, tracks from deer and raccoon at the water's edge. As the group crouches around a shallow
pool formed by a seep in the fractured rock, the farmer's grown
children yell like preschoolers. *Tadpoles!* The pool is no bigger
than my forearm, but as I move in for a closer look I discover a
ball of shiny, translucent foam teetering on the edge. It is a mass
of frog's eggs, camouflaged, vulnerable, and precious.

Most impressive are the plants that grow from impossibly narrow crevices. White mistflower (aka Havana snakeroot), wind-
blown and ragged, dots the landscape. Its roots twist, bend, and
squeeze between the layers of rock, reaching for the smallest
crumbs of soil. A yaupon holly stands knee high, its red berries
like a billboard, sure to capture the attention of mockingbirds and
migrating cedar waxwings. Agarita with its prickly, holly-like
leaves and butter-yellow flowers, a favorite of solitary bees, is in
bloom. It is known as the bread-and-honey shrub for its sweet
aroma that spreads through the air. Closer to the pools, seeps, and
waterfalls, maidenhair fern clings to canyon walls, roots hanging,
suspended in the air like the delicate tentacles of jellyfish.

I start to wonder if there is a branch of science that studies life
in the cracks. Later I learn that there are ecologists who investigate crevice communities. Some of the frequently noted residents of cracks are mosses, lichen, and sedges. There have also
been studies of animals that rely on crevices, such as barnacles,
crevice-nesting Alaskan seabirds called crested auklets, and flat,
desert-dwelling iguanas called chuckwallas. Remarkably, when
threatened, one such lizard, *Sauromalus obesus*, will wedge itself
into a crevice and overexpand its lungs. Crammed so tightly into
its hiding place, the chuckwalla cannot be removed.

Closer to home, a friend shared the story of a Texas madrone
tree, a rare and ancient species dating to prehistoric times. While
most madrone saplings fall victim to deer browsing, this tree took
root in a crack near Alligator Creek in Austin and survived.

Within the branching limestone cracks, all of these species seek shelter, a safe place to hide during challenging times. I scan the ledges hoping to find a space wide enough, deep enough, to hold my own body.

On the trail, I continue to photograph, record, sketch, acknowledge, and celebrate every living thing in the gorge as if it is some kind of biological victory. It is a victory, after all, to begin again from nothing.

Over the next five years after the birth of my third son my mother's body deteriorated at a rapid rate, giving her the appearance of someone much older. Her skin became like a fine layer of tissue paper, the network of veins and arteries so close to the surface that if you stood near her you could almost hear the blood pumping through her body. She bumped into furniture that had been in the same spot for years, and her skin bruised easily and often. A dedicated runner for most of her adult life, she had developed large, well-defined calf muscles that withered away. Soon she dropped from a size ten to a size two, no longer interested in eating more than a banana or a few bites of coffee ice cream. When we hugged, it felt as though her body would shatter into a million unrecognizable pieces.

Throughout her life, my mother had been a map person, always planning the next trip. Not long after she taught me to drive, we left from our home in Virginia and headed north to Maine, making sure to take the Capital Beltway, the Baltimore Harbor Tunnel, and the Tappan Zee Bridge—to conquer my fears of driving in unfamiliar territory, she said. Now she is afraid to leave her house, afraid of losing herself.

My mother's decision to keep her struggles with dementia a secret—from her closest friends, from her sisters, from her only child—tore through my life, leaving an enormous empty space. While I wanted to talk about the future and about her care, she wanted to talk about the toad who hunkered down in the bird-bath, the territorial hummingbird who reigned over the scarlet salvia, and the young black bear who cracked open the bird feeder. When she asked me to help her collect fallen tree limbs in the yard, we worked side by side in silence, stacking sticks and twigs into neat piles by the forest's edge.

Three years later, when cancer ravaged my uncle's body, our family discussed the situation, researched alternative treatments, and traveled to his home in California. We cooked Yorkshire pudding and roast beef with horseradish cream. For dessert I baked the lemon meringue pie while my mother sipped a glass of pinot noir. We stayed up late watching old videos of weddings and trips together to Hawaii, sinking into one another in the fluffy white cushions of an overstuffed couch. Then we said goodbye.

Dementia would be different.

When I visit with my mother, I search for what is missing and gather what is lost. I tuck those things away for later, like torn pieces of a map, hoping there will be enough left to navigate through the world without her.

As our tour group approaches the end of Canyon Gorge Trail, two bee brush trunks grow entwined where the floodwaters had wiped out a bridge and destroyed the road. The tree is not yet ready to bloom, but the buds hold the promise of the softest scent of tangerine. By early spring white flowers will overflow with nectar, nourishing thousands of bustling pollinators.

As I leave the gorge, I cling to the image of the flowering tree, its ability to flourish in a scarred landscape. I am hopeful that my mother and I will find a new way of being together in our own altered landscape.

FOLLOWING ROOTS

Blanco, Texas, September 27, 2019

The sun sears my skin as I scramble over a craggy hillside in search of hidden caves. For months the temperature has climbed toward one hundred degrees daily, and with less than an inch of rain since June, the land crumbles beneath my feet. As drought season grips Central Texas, life becomes unpredictable.

Three years ago, my husband, Bryant, and I bought this property—thirty acres of rundown ranchland with a spectacular sunset—at a time when we both needed somewhere to put down roots. During our twenty-year marriage, we had moved six times, and although the property doesn't have a house on it yet we live nearby and visit often. We plan to carve out a niche of our own on the rocky slopes and create habitat for plants and animals.

One day, while we were still getting to know the land, a neighbor approached us with a curious question: "Have you found the caves yet?" He didn't offer directions or even a hint about their location. Instead, he smiled, winked at my three sons, and sent us off on our own adventure.

That simple question marked the beginning of a family quest. Because we are originally from the East Coast, I wondered if we would know how to find a Texas cave, and after many failed attempts it dawned on me that perhaps we were searching in the wrong places.

* * *

While I continue exploring our property, I descend a steep slope into a canyon. A thin layer of broken limestone slips away beneath my feet. The soles of my shoes scrape the ground, startling me. My mind, which had been wandering with ghosts, focuses on the precarious situation. As I slide downhill on my bottom, my hands drag over sharp shards of stone, and I come to rest next to a stand of yucca plants. Their long pointed fronds, like swords, poke at my skin.

Scattered on the ground nearby, the withered leaves of a chinquapin oak form a thin blanket. In times of drought, these trees and many other species cling to life by shedding their leaves to conserve water. For survival, trees also rely on their extensive root systems that twist and turn, pushing through soil and rock in search of minute drops of water deep within the earth. I try to dig a hole in the dirt with my fingers and fail, realizing it would require a pickaxe to succeed. I marvel at the strength of roots.

Like the skeletal oak, my own family tree suffers, its bare branches exposed. Seven years ago, when I turned forty, my family started to disappear one by one. Cancer and pneumonia claimed aunts and uncles. My husband's stepfather died of complications from dementia. My father-in-law underwent surgeries for heart disease and prostate cancer, an ordeal that drained his energy from deep within. For many years my mother inhabited a world of her own, a victim of dementia, and my father declined rapidly after suffering through months of radiation treatment. Home alone, my mother-in-law tripped and fell onto a concrete patio. During a scan to assess her injuries, the radiologist discovered an aneurism hidden in her abdomen.

I spent weeks traveling across the country, returning to empty spaces—hotels, hospital rooms, and homes filled with boxes—witnessing layers of family history dissolve. The absence of loved ones, like gaping holes in our family's foundation, left me struggling to navigate an altered landscape.

CAVE WITHOUT A NAME

Boerne, Texas, October 5, 2019

> *How to find a cave, clue 1: Caves may exist underneath a dip in the terrain or a hole in the ground, or they may exist where a river simply vanishes.*

To learn more about locating caves, I decide to follow the roots that seem to know something about survival in a world of cracks and holes and darkness. I escape from the harsh reality of life aboveground and disappear, not fully aware of what I seek to unearth or where my subterranean journey will lead.

My first stop is a hole in the ground less than three feet wide. In 1929 a goat fell through the hole. While searching for his lost animal, a rancher stumbled upon the opening and, following the rescue, covered the hole with a boulder. For years the opening remained hidden in plain sight until three siblings, who were visiting the ranch, noticed steam rising from beneath the boulder. When they pushed it aside, they found themselves staring down a long, dark tunnel: the entrance to a cave.

It turns out that holes in the ground are not unusual in this part of Texas, known as the Hill Country. Millions of years ago, the land was covered by an ancient sea. As marine creatures died, their shells and skeletons accumulated on the ocean floor. Under pressure, they formed limestone, a soft porous rock. Then the sea receded. When carbon dioxide from the air mixed with rainwater, a weak acid was produced that trickled downward, dissolving rock and carving holes. With its honeycombed structure, limestone acted like a sponge, storing water in the holes. Holes and cracks expanded over long periods of time, until eventually cavities like the Cave without a Name were born.

I join a guide and a small group to start our descent. One hundred and twenty-six stone steps, the equivalent of eighteen stories, spiral down through a narrow tunnel. The lighting, as soft as candlelight, allows me to fade into the shadows. As I leave behind a world deprived of water and enter a world transformed by water, I tuck my head to avoid the low ceiling and stoop over in an awkward position. When I spread out my arms to steady myself, I touch the rough wavy layers of the cave walls, wet and cold. The rock envelops me like a protective layer, like a snail's shell, as I move deeper into the subterranean wilderness.

The change in temperature, to sixty-six degrees, is immediate, the constant, year-round temperature. Drips fall at irregular intervals, land with a gentle thud, and cool my skin. The walls glisten and sparkle, and my feet splash through shallow puddles. Water is everywhere. It seeps into the withered places deep inside of me. Within these walls, tears could fall unseen, merge with the underground waters, and be carried away.

Once we reach the cave's main room, I head to the edge of a shallow river. The river originates on the surface of a neighboring property and flows downstream. To my left, it enters the cave through a two-inch gap in the bottom of the rock wall. To my right, the river makes a sharp turn and heads about three more miles underground and then out of the cave, merging again with the Guadalupe River on the surface. As water on the surface evaporates, this water is stored and protected deep within the earth.

This type of waterway, one that travels back and forth between the surface and the subterranean, is called a disappearing river.

Last summer my family and I sprinkled my mother's ashes in the bay by our cabin on the Maine coast. She had died suddenly after suffering from a stroke. At sunset we huddled on the beach near a large rock, the one my sons had nicknamed the pirate ship rock. It was the same rock where, many years ago, Mom had shared a secret with me. As we knelt on the soft, slippery mounds of seaweed, she encouraged me to peer underneath the rock's ledge.

There, rare lavender sea stars and creamy white snail eggs hung like miniature stalagmites. As the brilliant colors of the sunset faded from the sky, we watched as the waves carried my mother home to the sea.

I thought we were done with loss, with emptiness, with holes and cracks, and missing people. I was wrong.

CAVES AT JACOB'S WELL

Wimberley, Texas, October 10, 2019

> *How to find a cave, clue 2: Elaborate cave systems may exist beneath a river or a creek.*

The caves at Jacob's Well, often referred to as death traps, are the second stop on my subterranean journey. Unlike the Cave without a Name, exploring this cave system requires special equipment, training, and permits because it is submerged beneath Cypress Creek.

The well, a popular swimming hole, is actually an enormous cave entrance and the site of an artesian spring. When water deep within the earth becomes trapped between rocks and rainwater continues to enter the system, pressure builds. The water rushes to the surface and escapes. Sometimes springs look like tiny bubbles in the silt and at other times they are more forceful, expelling gallons of water per day. The spring is the source of Cypress Creek and the lifeblood of the surrounding communities.

Peering down over a limestone ledge, I spot the hole, which could easily be overlooked. Shaped like an enormous eyeball, it stares back at me from beneath the clear, cool waters. Long strands of lime-green algae surround the opening of the hole, which is about four times larger than a manhole cover. Several bass species swim near the spring and along the riverbanks. They have returned to spawn. As I gaze down from the ledge, I cannot see the bottom of the submerged tunnel beneath the hole. It descends for thirty feet. The tunnel appears to narrow as it disappears into the depths, and the water darkens from crystal blue to midnight blue, the color of the sky before a storm.

The interaction between the surface and what lies below is critical to survival. Here, and at other springs around the Hill Country, the protected subterranean waters return to the surface, to the dry and forgotten places.

In 2016 a local group of professional divers filmed and mapped the interior as part of the Jacob's Well Exploration Project. Their investigation revealed that after plunging straight down into the hole—a feat that requires tremendous effort due to the strong flow—one finds two tunnels, each a little less than a mile long and fourteen stories underground. It takes five hours roundtrip to travel through one tunnel.

The passages are dark and, at times, impossibly narrow. At the end of one underwater room is a challenging passageway appropriately named the Birth Canal. The conditions are characterized by unstable terrain (shifting rubble) and silt. Disturbed silt can cause a diver to become disoriented and lose her way in the darkness. Despite the danger, something powerful draws people to the caves of Jacob's Well.

Scientists visit caves, springs, and wells, searching for unique life forms. The tiny cracks, tunnels, and larger voids provide layers of unique habitat, perfect places for plants and animals to live. As it turns out, the Hill Country aquifers are home to many unusual species, both terrestrial and aquatic, that can only be found living in and around the Edwards-Trinity aquifer system. Texas blind salamanders, for example, with their see-through bodies, tiny limbs, tadpole-like tails, and crimson gills protruding like wings from their necks, were once believed to be juvenile dragons. An abundance of snail species, their delicate, translucent shells smaller than a grain of rice, also thrives in these areas. Catfish the size of my little finger, shrimp, and other invertebrates lack eyes and pigmentation. They swim like watery ghosts through the limestone chambers. Here, life adapts to darkness.

Jean Krejca, an Austin-based speleologist, or cave scientist, whose research focuses on subterranean species, says that what draws her to the world belowground is the thrill of the unknown. "There's no remote detection technique [like maps or aerial photos]," she explains. "There's no way to know what's around the next corner, but to physically go around that next corner." In this field, fear is often the precursor to discovery.

In 2000, for the first time in recorded history, the artesian spring at Jacob's Well ran dry. Then it happened again—five more times in the past eleven years. More than one hundred private wells also ran dry. Cypress Creek itself was reduced to a trickle. Yet the spring had survived the worst drought on record in 1950. What had changed? With the onset of explosive growth and development, more and more wells are being drilled. There is also pressure from commercial industries eager to pump, transport, and sell the spring water, a plan that appeals to a handful of private landowners.

The surrounding communities express concern for the future. They fear that there are too many straws in the aquifer, a situation that can lead to overdraft. This happens when demand is too high, not allowing enough time for rainfall to recharge the aquifer. Like us, the natural world needs time to heal.

Last week I received another phone call in the early morning hours. My cousin had returned to our family cabin in Maine, an annual trip he took with his brother and two friends. He had sat down to a lobster dinner, stood up, and collapsed. He was fifty-seven years old.

We assumed it was a heart attack, although an autopsy wasn't performed. He wasn't sick. He wasn't overweight. It was genetics, and it had happened before. Our grandfather, at fifty-nine, had collapsed on the golf course. DNA, with its deadly mutations, wrapped itself around the branches of our family tree like a serpent lurking in the shadows.

Until then, the losses had followed a natural progression, devastating but not unexpected. In the days after the news, Bryant and I rushed to schedule doctor appointments and update our wills. I received boxes filled with the remnants of other lives and found spaces for new things, reminders. At night I checked Bryant's breathing as he slept and fought the urge to gather my sons, hold them close, shelter them. At least then, for a moment, I could pretend they were safe.

Outside the land was still brittle, devastated by the extended drought. Giant wind gusts swept across the prairie, shook the house, and scattered broken oak limbs, like bodies, on the ground. I waited and dreamt of caves.

LADY BIRD JOHNSON WILDFLOWER CENTER

Austin, October 31, 2019

> *How to find a cave, clue 3: Caves may have been hidden on purpose, filled in with dirt, rocks, and other debris, but sometimes a discovery happens when you least expect it.*

The third stop on my subterranean journey comes when something unusual captures my attention on a hiking trail. I pull out my binoculars and focus on a boxlike object in the middle of the prairie grasses, still brown and lifeless from the drought. Later, when I ask about it, the biologist's mysterious response suggests that the object is a cave marker. I smile to myself. Another cave reveals itself, this time by accident.

I find the latest copy of the Lady Bird Johnson Wildflower Center's magazine on a table in the visitor's center. The words "Crickets and Texas Caves" in small print at the bottom corner of the cover draw me in. It turns out that scientists have been restoring two caves, Wildflower Cave and La Crosse Cave, on the property.

In the past caves were filled in to prevent the loss of livestock, like the goat in Boerne, and to trap water on the surface for stock ponds and mill activities. Other projects, like highway construction, also harm the subterranean ecosystem. When a void is encountered, piles of rubble, gravel, and sand are dumped into the cracks and caves below, to fill in the empty spaces and make the surface more stable. And then construction resumes, permanently disrupting the water pathways in these already shattered places, a change that will disturb habitat and interfere with the aquifers' ability to store, protect, and provide water.

I feel empathy for these underground places that teeter on the edge of tremendous loss and upheaval. The sense of helplessness when confronted with unwanted change is familiar, and I wonder how the land will respond.

At the wildflower center, cave restoration began with an excavation project. Scientists and volunteers removed trash, rubble, mulch, soil, and fencing from the caves. Then the restoration crew planted trees, shrubs, and grasses to provide food for animals that leave the caves to forage, like crickets and harvestmen (aka daddy longlegs). The plants' roots also stabilized the soil, preventing erosion near the cave entrances. Then the scientists and volunteers waited.

Before long life returned to the caves. Animals like bobcats, ringtails, and porcupines were observed coming and going, using the caves as a refuge to escape stressful conditions such as drought and extreme heat. This was a familiar strategy, one that reminded me of how I felt when the cool water droplets fell on my skin inside the Cave without a Name.

Other species took up permanent residence. Millipedes, spiders, ground beetles, and harvestmen were spotted. Speleologists also encountered populations of cliff chirping frogs and western slimy salamanders living in the wet regions of the caves. And this year, for the first time, five tricolored bats arrived to hibernate in Wildflower Cave. There is hope that they will return next year and the population will continue to grow.

Blanco, Texas, November 1, 2019

After learning more about what lies beneath the Hill Country, I gather my family to search for caves on our property, optimistic that today is the day we will find them. We hike until we reach a large depression in the ground at the base of a cliff. Near a dry riverbed, a pile of boulders appears to have been strategically placed, and our excitement grows. We push the rocks aside. No holes. No tunnels. Our quest continues.

Moving forward, our family plans to restore habitat and enhance water pathways, a project that will include planting native prairie grasses. Their strong, interwoven root system will help capture soil and water, preventing loss. It is a project that will take more than a lifetime. And, of course, we will keep searching for holes and caves. But for now, the image of life beneath my feet—of roots, creatures, and water sheltered in undisturbed places—brings me peace.

The crack and boom of thunder followed by an eerie silence and a sudden gust of wind prompt us to take cover. And then a long-forgotten sound breaks the silence: the pounding of rain falling in heavy sheets against the scorched ground. I inhale the raw, earthy smell of wet soil. Finally. I imagine the water coursing through the hidden pathways that cover the earth's surface like blood vessels: weaving through the tall dried grasses and pooling over the limestone outcrop tucked beneath a clump of prickly pear cacti; filtering down into the soil, bathing the roots of the prairie grasses as it flows; down farther, pushing through cracks and crevices, seeping into caves; and deeper still until it reaches the salamanders, frogs, and fish that wait in dark places.

As the rain brings relief to the land, the shifting silt and rubble settles and I emerge from my own subterranean journey, ready for life to return. I understand now that the holes, cracks, and disturbed layers—the darkest places within myself—are not empty after all; they do not echo with the whispers of absence as I had feared. Instead they form passageways where stories and memories, like water, flow through me. And I am meant to return and explore those challenging places from time to time, to disappear like the river that moves back and forth between the surface and the subterranean.

I exhale. It is time to rest, to heal. For now.

TANGLED LEGS

The tangled mass, wedged into a golf-ball-sized hole in a rock wall, looks like a hairball, like something you might find left behind in the shower drain. Curious, I move in closer. Is it some sort of stringy worm or the roots of a plant? While I ponder the possibilities, the mass begins to pulse. Within seconds, black spindly legs, twisting and turning, work desperately to free themselves, limb by limb. And then hundreds of daddy longlegs pour out of the hole and scurry off in every direction.

This is not my first encounter with daddy longlegs. I have had a lifelong fascination with creatures we forget to see. In college I studied biology, an excuse to continue exploring odd and out-of-the-way places. I have observed daddy longlegs in rotting logs, under rocks, and in leaf litter. They are homebodies, keeping to themselves and rarely venturing out. I have never known them to be social, like ants, but seeing them huddled together makes me question whether there is more to their story.

Most people are surprised to learn that daddy longlegs are not spiders. Scorpions are actually a more closely related species. Like spiders and scorpions, daddy longlegs are arachnids and have eight segmented legs. But daddy longlegs do not build webs or inject venom into their prey. They are nocturnal scavengers, feeding on decomposing material and the occasional live insect. Their head and body segments are fused, giving them a globular appearance, and their eyes are perched on top of two projections, like horns. But it is often their delicate, oversized legs that are their most recognizable feature.

In order to learn more about the species of daddy longlegs that live in Texas, I drive north to Austin to meet with Alex Wild, curator of entomology for the University of Texas Biodiversity Center. I park in front of a nondescript building made of blood-red brick. Inside, faded cartoon images of butterflies, caterpillars, and other insects dangle from cinder block walls, an attempt to breathe life into the otherwise sterile environment.

I glance at a scrap of paper with a room number scribbled on it and set out to find Wild. After poking my head into several rooms, I notice a pattern: stacks of drawers containing preserved butterflies, beetles, and other creepy-crawlies cover every surface. A slightly off-putting odor—a mixture of damp wood and decay—hangs in the air. Suddenly I am acutely aware of the absence of human beings. Much to my relief, after ten minutes I find Wild sitting in his cocoon-like office, hunched over the computer.

A burnt orange UT T-shirt hangs behind him. The university's beloved mascot, Bevo the longhorn bull, has been replaced by a longhorn beetle. As is common in the field of entomology, people are identified by the species that consume their lives. Wild studies ant behavior; he is the ant man. He is also a photographer who believes passionately that "little things matter." Here, he is an entomological librarian overseeing a collection with more than 2 million specimens.

As we wander down a narrow hallway, we discuss a source of misinformation: names. The common name, daddy longlegs, is confusing because other unrelated species like cellar spiders or crane flies are also called daddy longlegs. And much to my surprise, some daddy longlegs don't even have long legs; they have short legs that are built for digging. For that reason, the term "harvestmen" is preferred, originating from the fact that they are active during the harvest season. But as Wild points out, we shouldn't forget that there are female daddy longlegs too. He suggests the name "harvest people," revealing an oddly appealing entomological humor that is beginning to emerge. To avoid confusion, scientists use the name of the taxonomic order they belong to, Opiliones. It is a lovely name that rolls off the tongue like something Italian and delicious.

Wild unlocks a heavy metal door, and we enter a space the size of a walk-in closet. This is where the wet collection is housed, he explains. Insects with sturdier exoskeletons, like beetles, are part of the pin collection—the drawers I passed while lost in the maze of classrooms. The more fragile specimens are preserved in a mixture of water and ethanol. The scene unfolds like a series of Russian nesting dolls: metal shelves lining the room from floor to ceiling, each shelf stacked with glass jars, each jar filled with vials of creatures.

We squeeze through cramped spaces, careful not to knock anything over, and head to the Cave Arthropod and Invertebrate Collection at the back of the room. In Texas, there are at least three thousand caves and sinkholes; it is like living atop a hidden world made of rocky Swiss cheese. The terrain, which geologists refer to as a karst landscape, is ideal for creatures that inhabit cracks, crevices, and cavities, including mosses, lichen, cacti, and lizards. These are the same damp, dark places where Opiliones go about their lives.

Wild pulls down jar after jar, lifts them up to the light, and turns them around and around in his hands. Sometimes it is difficult to see inside because the labels obscure the contents. The labels contain information like dates, locations, and names of scientists and species. Nearby, coiled centipedes, the size of small snakes, float in clear liquid. Behind me, whip scorpions bigger than my hand— one per jar—display their armored undersides. Wild points out that there are specimens here that haven't been studied. In fact, there are probably new undescribed species or species that may have already disappeared just sitting on the shelves.

At least twenty jars contain Opiliones of various shapes and sizes. Most are named for the places where they were discovered, like the Bee Creek cave harvestman. Unlike the enormous Opiliones that live in rainforests and display striking color combinations of black, mint green, and fluorescent yellow, these cave dwellers are tiny ghostly white creatures. Most surprising is the Bone Cave harvestman, its cantaloupe-colored body no bigger than my fingernail.

All of these species are part of an ecosystem that is threatened by rapid development and changing environmental conditions. Because the subterranean is a place we don't think about often, and because it seems remote, we fail to realize the changes that occur beneath our feet. "As Central Texas becomes hotter, species from Mexico move north, and as it becomes drier, species shift to the eastern part of the state," Wild explains. One reason these collections are significant is that they allow for comparison over time, a way to document change.

But much of the collection is what Wild refers to as "entomological dark matter." Like the unidentified Opiliones species sitting on shelves, there are mountains of specimens waiting to be sorted in cabinets, drawers, containers, and vials that line the floors and shelves, room after room. It is hard to comprehend what we stand to lose when we don't recognize what already exists.

Before I leave Wild makes one last stop to introduce me to Whippy McWhipface, an African whip scorpion. Until today, I had only read about these unusual creatures. They hide on cave walls, so still and so well camouflaged that people are unaware of their existence. Carefully reaching into a plastic terrarium, Wild turns over a piece of bark to reveal a flat, seemingly faceless, kite-shaped creature clinging to the bottom. It reminds me of a horseshoe crab.

Whippy exhibits a difficult personality: moody, unpredictable, and fast. Wild assures me that he has no intention of spending the rest of the day searching for Whippy, so he quickly stuffs the whip scorpion back inside the terrarium and slams the lid shut. Something in Wild's voice makes me suspect that, around here, escapes are common. I watch my step on the way out.

To learn more about Opiliones in the wild and to uncover the mystery of the whirling mass, I contact Jacob Owen, an ecologist who works for the Zara Environmental Group in Austin. He spends his days in the dark recesses of caves, collecting and recording the living things that he encounters. Many of Owen's specimens can be found in Wild's collection. Zara Environmental is hired to do biological surveys by the Texas Department of Transportation and other developers before the start of a construction project, before the subterranean habitat is shattered. While Owen is not a harvestmen specialist, he has been up close and personal with countless Opiliones.

According to Owen, the caves where Opiliones live are extreme environments that are difficult to study. In a report prepared for the Texas Department of Fish and Wildlife, researchers at Zara Environmental describe their sites as places defined by "constricted crawlways, vertical drops, low oxygen levels, an abundance of mesocaverns or cracks and voids that are inaccessible to humans." Another challenge is trying to count secretive species in the dark. And while the scientists have an idea of the numbers and types of species, they know little about the range, life span, feeding habits, or behavior of individual species. As Owen admits, "The farther down we go, the less we know."

I describe the mass of tangled legs in the rock wall and ask Owen if he has ever seen such a sight. *Of course!* Tangles, estimated to contain millions of individuals, hang from cave entrances, especially in the spring. Sometimes they are as big as basketballs. They are common not only in Texas but in karst terrain all over the world.

Owen is careful to differentiate between the two major types of Opiliones. Some are species, like the ones in Wild's collection, that live their entire lives in subterranean caves (troglobites). Others, like the ones I saw in the rock wall, use cave entrances and cracks near the surface as shelters (trogloxenes), scrambling in and out in search of food. They are typically the ones that form gigantic masses and, in Texas, are usually *Leiobunum townsendi*, a species that lacks a common name. The cave-dwelling species, it turns out, do not gather in clusters, preferring a solitary existence.

But why do *Leiobunum townsendi* form massive clusters? It has to do with defense. A mass appears more dangerous to predators than an individual. And when the members of the mass begin to pulse in unison, it is intimidating. To fend off predators, each individual Opilione is also capable of secreting a foul-smelling fluid that is composed of more than sixty chemicals. And of course, the bigger the mass, the bigger the smell.

As I head home with a growing list of questions, Opiliones creep deeper into my imagination. It amazes me to think that these creatures have been exploring the earth—all of its remote cracks, crevices, and voids—for more than 400 million years. They exist in places where we cannot go, that we will never see. And they know this planet in ways that we will never know. As their ancient world shifts and the silence of the subterranean is lost, I wonder what stories Opiliones will have to tell.

REWILDING

On hands and knees, I squeeze through a triangular puka (hole) and push through a dark, cramped six-foot-long tunnel. My shins and forearms are smeared with grit, the same rust color as the mud; sweat drips down my face. It took my family an hour to reach this spot on the southern coast of Kauai. Along the way, our teenagers made dramatic mock complaints, and our seven-year-old gave not-so-subtle hints about heading to the beach. But as the adrenaline pumps through my body, I know I have made the right choice. I squirm out of the tunnel, stand up, and gaze around at the crumbling remains of Hawaii's largest limestone cave: Makauwahi Cave.

For the past six months, I had been obsessed with limestone—its cracks, crevices, and caves. My home in Central Texas sits atop limestone, layers upon layers of ancient seashells and saltwater skeletons that have turned to stone. As a curious ecologist, I spent hours researching and exploring those mysterious subterranean spaces. Now, far from home, a limestone cave—or what remained of the cave—beckoned me. Although my family wanted to go kayaking, I knew I had to find the cave ruins. I knew the hidden world beneath my feet had a way of revealing secrets.

The journey began on a paved backroad that ended abruptly; then the island's wilderness sprawled out before us. Jarring potholes the size of dinosaur footprints and coal-black rocks protruded from the narrow, dirt road at every bend. Kauai is the oldest Hawaiian island (estimated to be 5 million years old) and the most remote of the chain. Overgrown grasses, vines, and tree limbs crept closer, scraping the sides of our van, as if they were trying to entrap us.

The majority of plants we passed were introduced, carried to the island by wind, wings (bats and birds), and waves (humans in boats). Once established, seeds spread and saplings sprouted in the nutrient-rich soil, growing with abandon—another reminder of our close proximity to one of the wettest spots on the planet, Mount Waialeale.

We set out on the next leg of the journey on foot. The winding, muddy path veered uphill, and I noticed that the vegetation began to change. The dense shrubbery had been cleared and replaced by patches of disturbed soil and evenly spaced holes, suggesting this was a garden. Everywhere I looked bright green plants— miniature palm trees and succulents—popped out of the ground. Loving hands had been hard at work, but who had been there and why?

I bent down to read the metal plaques, letting my family move on without me. Each one contained three names that identified the plant: the Hawaiian name, the scientific name, and the common name. As I read their names out loud, the words swirled through the air like floral poetry: wiliwili, naupaka papa, akia, lonomea, ohelo ai, loulu. The words felt like a greeting at a gathering of new friends.

Groundcover, shrubs, and saplings—almost all of the plants that surrounded me were native to the island, according to the markers. Some, shaped like artichokes, had leaves that were thick, water-filled, and spongy; others had leaves that were thin, needle-like, and rough, like sandpaper. Many had fanlike fronds, broad with raised veins and ridges, that crinkled like dried newspaper. Although this was a young plant community, I imagined this spot in the future: a prehistoric garden with trees towering over my head, a rainbow of dangling fruits and flowers, and enormous drooping seedpods rattling in the wind. I closed my eyes, breathed in the sweet, salty air, and settled deeper into the soil.

"Don't forget to look for the puka," I yelled ahead, trying to catch up with my family. Then, distracted by distant voices from far below, I peeked over the edge of a cliff into a sinkhole the size of a basketball arena. This was where the cave's main room would have been, before the ceiling collapsed seven thousand years ago. All that remained were the cave's jagged walls and the exposed anatomy of a shattered subterranean labyrinth.

In order to explore the cave ruins, I would still have to find the elusive puka, hidden somewhere along the towering ring of rock, the protector of Makauwahi's buried secrets.

Down the steep slope and around the corner, my son spots a keyhole-shaped crack in the rock wall. After sliding sideways through the crack and crawling along a muddy tunnel floor, I enter what is left of the cave's main room, blue sky overhead. With the space surrounded by ancient tree species like kou and loulu palms, it is like passing through a portal to the past.

Across the grassy field, my family and I approach a slightly larger hole in the wall, one of the smaller rooms in the cave system that is still standing. The dark space is the size of a bedroom. We don't get far before signs stop us from wandering any farther. These passageways into the rocky interior are ceremonial spaces and burial caves, sacred to the Native Hawaiians. And beneath these sacred places, fragile limestone habitats are home to rare invertebrate species, including amphipods, isopods, and blind wolf spiders, creatures unique to this site.

In contrast to the serene setting we encounter today, extreme events over the past millions of years, some catastrophic and others gradual, have shaped the land: volcano eruptions, hurricanes, floods, tsunamis, and erosion. The Makauwahi cave system started to develop four hundred thousand years ago. Sand, which formed as waves pounded and crushed the surrounding coral reefs, washed to shore. Wind blew the sand inland and then piled it into massive sand mountains. Over time, vegetation blanketed the dunes. Then fresh water and salt water mixed with the sand and decomposing plant material, eventually transforming the dunes themselves into petrified limestone fossils.

As rainwater trickled down over the stone, dripping farther into the cracks and crevices, an acid formed. The acid slowly dissolved the limestone, leaving behind smaller voids and larger caves. Later, sand and rock blocked the entrances and exits around the sinkhole, which filled with water. After the cave ceiling collapsed, the sinkhole filled with fresh water, forming a lake that remained until the mid-twentieth century.

As we prepare to leave the cave ruins through the puka, we pass a shallow pool where the remains of a bullfrog lie submerged. The frog's skin has peeled away and disappeared. Soon decomposition will claim the tendons and other tissues too, and the pile of bones will be lost under layers of sediment. We are witness to the birth of a modern-day fossil.

It turns out that the Makauwahi Cave system, including the crumbling caves, tunnels, and sinkhole, is a hotspot for fossils. Decomposing plant material and other soft sediment accumulate, deposited by surface water flowing over the land, creating the perfect environment for fossil formation. Just as I had hoped, the subterranean world is beginning to reveal its secrets.

In 1992 paleoecologist David Burney and his wife, Lida Burney, arrived in Kauai to unearth the fossils. As they sifted and mucked through the layers of sediment, they used their data to paint a picture of the environment at different times throughout history, including the time before humans arrived on the island. They concluded that the ecology of the island had changed drastically over time, transformed by human activity.

For nearly thirty years the Burneys excavated fossils of insects, birds, and mammals, but they were most fascinated by the microscopic fossils of seeds and pollen. They examined the seeds and analyzed the pollen spores under microscopes. By the end of the excavation project, they had produced long lists of native plant species, and then they returned to reintroduce those plants, a process known as rewilding.

The goal of the Burneys' work was to nurture a healthier and more diverse ecosystem, something that happens when native plant species outnumber introduced species. But would it be possible to use the fossil record as a guide to encourage the growth of species that hadn't flourished here in hundreds of years?

In order to answer that question, the Burneys leased seventeen acres of land surrounding the cave and got to work in their living laboratory, the Makauwahi Cave Preserve. They relied on assistance from conservation organizations, local arborists, botanists, school groups, scout groups, and other volunteers. They paid special attention to relationships, bringing together local elders with younger generations. While they all worked side by side, plant wisdom and island ecology were shared through stories.

The volunteers collected native seeds and raised plants in pots. Then they placed the seedlings in the soil and tended the saplings, like the ones I had seen along the garden path. The Burneys also introduced sulcata tortoises to browse on the invasive weeds. The tortoises mimicked the foraging behavior of giant ducks and geese, species that were now extinct. For ten years the volunteers did this again and again in the bog, the estuary, and the abandoned agricultural field near the remains of the cave system. After much trial and error, more than eighty plant species survived and began to reproduce on their own, covering the seventeen-acre preserve in living fossils.

A unique aspect of the Makauwahi project is that, as volunteers restored the surface habitat, something unexpected was happening in the dark, remote places underground. Near caves, three plants—Hawaiian caper, velvetleaf, and kumakani—flourished, their strong, water-seeking roots pushing down into the rocky crevices. There the roots secreted a nutritious fluid that fed expanding colonies of bacteria and fungi. As these microscopic populations exploded, invertebrates, like the colorless amphipods and isopods, arrived in shallow pools where they were hunted by blind wolf spiders. Roots that descended from the surface, it turns out, laid the foundation for the subterranean food web, shedding light on the critical connection between life on the surface and what lies below.

I recognize the Burneys' passion, their desire to connect people, plants, and places and to dig deeper beneath the surface. When my husband and I moved from the East Coast to Texas, I immersed myself in a small-scale restoration project, transforming our backyard into wildlife habitat.

I started by scattering native grass and wildflower seed. For the tree and shrub layer, I planted mountain laurel, cedar elm, and live oak. The next spring I removed huisache saplings and prickly pear cacti that threatened to take over and crowd out other species. Soon the animals, from earthworms to moths to armadillos, made themselves at home. The bird population grew too, with the arrival of bluebirds, painted buntings, Baltimore orioles, vermilion flycatchers, and flocks of cedar waxwings.

But over time johnsongrass and other invasive plants sprung from the soil, their stubborn root systems and prolific reproductive strategies making them nearly impossible to remove. I admit, there have been days I felt defeated, and on occasion I have considered mowing it all down.

Would it be possible to rid an entire island of invasive species and restore the island's ecosystem? After all, I struggle to keep just one acre thriving. Plus, several nonnative vine species on Kauai can engulf an entire house in a matter of months. And even if the native plants were somehow reintroduced across the island, would the eroded soil contain the proper amounts of minerals and nutrients to support them?

I find my answer at the airport as we prepare to leave the island. On the way to our gate, I pass a display for another restoration project taking place at the Huleia estuary. Volunteers there are clearing acres of red mangrove trees from wetland ecosystems, places that have deteriorated into swamps of stagnant, foul-smelling water. It is a difficult, time-consuming process. Acre by acre, the volunteers dig up thick roots from choked waterways, allowing water to flow freely once again and the fish, plants, and other living things to return.

But it is a quote that holds me, transfixed: "Malama ia Huleia, Maiama Huleia," which translates to "Care for Huleia, Huleia will care for you."

In the end, it isn't about how quickly the work is done or even how much acreage is covered. The value of the work is in the action—people kneeling on the ground together, placing their hands deep in the soil. It is as much a rewilding of human beings as it is a restoration of the island.

At home I return to my own work, my own wild place. I kneel close to the ground, tuck sage roots into a hole and cover them with handfuls of limestone soil. As the afternoon fades, sunlight falls on my skin, illuminating the dirt ingrained in the cracked pathways of my fingertips. My mind returns to Kauai's rust-colored soil: I see that broken places and empty spaces, where things collapse and all seems lost, are places where people can return to dig deeper, to uncover what has long been hidden. To begin again.

FINDING HOME
FAR AWAY

One thousand miles from home, you find yourself displaced—removed from granite cliffs, birch trees, and bogs. Uprooted.

You live in the central time zone now, far from family. When winter rains fall, paved streets flood. No one tells you that you should stay inside.

It is year five of marriage. Your husband dresses in scrubs, leaves before sunrise, returns after the rest of the world is asleep.

Outside, lost in the maze of the suburban terrain, human-sized reptiles lurk near strip malls and trees grow in tidy rows; snakes of all sizes slither through the bayous and into garages; owls shout their nocturnal hoots from rooftops, and minibeasts with crunchy exteriors roll dung across driveways, over and over.

All of these creatures possess familiar forms, but they are strangers with names you do not know.

When you are pregnant, you pace laminate floors in rooms that smell of paint. The backyard is a postage stamp of Saint Augustine grass with four copycat houses that peek over the fence. You gaze out the window.

You wait; nothing happens—not even a blue jay or a chickadee or some other ordinary bird comes to perch on a branch.

Soon wilderness, the kind that spills over roadsides with goldenrod and fireweed and blackberry vines, creeps into your dreams.

When the weather warms, you buy a lemon tree in a pot. The twiglike trunk is as tall as your three-year-old son, and the fruit's bumpy, bright skin mirrors his exuberant smile. He pokes at caterpillars on the leaves beneath his nose. They look like bird poop. You watch as one dangles upside down and pulls up the covers of its chrysalis.

You memorize poems by Pattiann Rogers. Hermit crabs and horned lizards skitter across the verses. In your mind, you are the one "Rolling Naked in the Morning Dew" with the taste of wild blueberries on your tongue. Pattiann reminds you that "home is wherever the people [you] love live." You scrawl it on a piece of packing paper and tape it to the wall, and when it peels away you tape it up again.

Years later, you leave.

This time you move a hundred miles west to scrub forests, prairie grasses, aquifers, and caves. The roads wind up and down scraggy limestone hills and over creeks. When you open the car window, it smells like woodsmoke. You arrive and step out onto a rock-covered possibility.

First you sift seeds from brown paper bags and sprinkle them on the soil. Then you mow a path. In the winter months, you study field guides.

When the weather warms, you plant okra and peas for your sons to pick. For the mockingbirds, you plant yaupon holly with juicy red berries and elm trees for nests. You place three bluebird houses along the path and an owl house on the oak's highest limb. You discover that leafcutter bees love rock rose. For the fritillary caterpillars, you plant passionflower vines, and for the swallow-tail caterpillars, you plant pipe vine and rue. You leave piles of leaves for the cecropia moths who overwinter in their cocoons. And for the ruby-throated hummingbirds, you prepare fields of red: honeysuckle, hibiscus, and salvia. As the weather cools, you build brush piles, shelter for families of lizards and hares.

And then you wait.

As you leaf through a well-worn book by Robin Wall Kimmerer, you remember copying her words into your journal. When the pages were filled, you copied them into the next journal and the next. You whisper to Robin, tell her now you know that "eutrophic old woman" who spends her days with butterflies and birds and bees, and you promise to continue planting long after your own children are gone.

Later, when you find yourself hiding from an enemy smaller than a cell or a pollen grain or a spore, you read about loneliness— how it causes cells to change and send danger signals to the brain, how the effects linger in bodies long after the feelings have passed.

Outside, two green anoles share a sunspot on the windowsill, and a butterfly, a cloudless sulfur, lands on a salvia's spiky blooms.

In their company, you are less lonely.

LEARNING THE SECRETS OF PRAIRIES

Anybody can love the mountains, but it takes soul to love the prairie.
— WILLA CATHER

Last year my neighbor set his yard on fire. I was returning from a trip to the store and, as soon as I opened the car door, an intense wave of hot, thick smoke hit me. It wasn't the pleasant scent of woodsmoke or barbecue, the smell that lingers in the Texas air regardless of season or time of day. But blazing brush piles, full of leaves and tree limbs, are not unusual either, so I wasn't alarmed at first.

I carried the grocery bags inside and set them on the kitchen counter. An eerie silence had settled over the house. As I searched for the rest of my family, something through the kitchen window caught my eye. Two houses down and across the cul-de-sac, knee-high orange flames raged, spreading swiftly across the front yard.

When I was a young, a neighbor's house had burned to the ground, and the family had moved away. The image of the abandoned lot had haunted me; there had been nothing left but the scorched trees, like skeletons rising from the ashes. Everything disappeared, as if the family had never existed. After that, whenever I heard sirens in the neighborhood, I hid. Now, with flames edging closer to my own home, thoughts raced through my mind: Should I dial 9-1-1? Should I yell for my husband and children, load them into the car, and speed away?

I grabbed my binoculars from the windowsill, hoping to gather more information. I rarely drove down that street, and I didn't know the owners of the house. Surprisingly, unlike the other manicured turfgrass lawns in the neighborhood, this yard, like mine, was a natural prairie, a mishmash of tall grasses and wildflowers.

A fit middle-aged man, with his jeans tucked into his cowboy boots, stood in the driveway. He used a long-handled digging shovel to move embers from the burned lawn on one side of the driveway to the active burn site on the other side of the driveway. Flames consumed the tall grasses, and their withered blades disintegrated before my eyes. Blue plastic buckets, which I hoped held water, lined the driveway. The man continued working, moving back and forth, back and forth. I listened for their sirens, but the fire trucks never came.

Every now and then, I returned to the window. The fire burned for several more hours until all that remained was charred earth.

What would compel someone to do such a thing, I wondered. Why would my neighbor put our families and our homes at risk? I never imagined that one day soon, I would consider burning the tall grasses in my own yard.

"There's a snake!" my seven-year-old son, Ryland, yells as he bursts into the house. I grab my phone from the table and hurry out the door. We jog from the driveway down the white-pebbled path that winds through the native grasses—some waist-high, others towering over Ryland's head. Midmorning on a spring day, our backyard thrums with the chitter-chatter of birds and the skitter-scatter of insects.

Ryland points to a patch of wildflowers. A thin lime-green ribbon, a little longer than my forearm, slithers along, taking her time, absorbing her surroundings. As I inch closer, I kneel on the warm ground and wait.

Then, at just the right moment, I snap the shot. My phone's camera captures the snake as she lifts her body, gradually entwining herself around several long, thick blades of eastern gama grass, a native plant that forms wide bunches. As she climbs higher, the butter-yellow scales of her underbelly shimmer, wet with morning dew.

I upload the photo to iNaturalist, a citizen science app that collects data for scientific research projects, and within seconds I receive an identification: a rough green snake, a nonvenomous creature that feeds on insects, snails, and tree frogs. *Yes!* I turn to Ryland and give him a thumbs-up. He grins. To our growing list, we add the rough green snake, another species who shares our home in the tall grasses—a vanishing habitat.

Several months after my neighbor set fire to his yard, I traveled to the world-renowned Missoula Fire Lab in Montana. As part of a group of science writers from Johns Hopkins University, I spent the day with fire ecologists. In addition to developing practices to prevent uncontrolled wildfires, the scientists studied the benefits of controlled, prescribed burns for land and habitat management.

Following a tour of the lab, we boarded a rundown yellow school bus and drove to the Lolo National Forest, where the U.S. Forest Service had regularly conducted low-intensity fires to manage the pine, fir, and birch habitat. I mentally prepared myself during the bumpy ride up the twisty mountain roads. I imagined standing amid a devastated landscape; I imagined the sound of my footsteps crunching across scorched ground; I imagined the stillness.

Instead, along the steep slope of Blue Mountain, I found myself lifting my feet, fearful of crushing tufts of brilliant green grasses and miniature stands of scraggly saplings. Branchless ponderosa pine trunks, like slender giants, reached toward the sky until, at the highest point, their needles dangled from spindly limbs. Dappled sunlight peeked through, and the fresh, memory-filled scent of pine seeped into my skin and followed me through the forest.

Near the mountain's peak, patches of lupine danced, their tall stems jiggling and bending as bees swarmed the clusters of indigo blossoms. Centipedes, millipedes, and pill bugs crawled over the charred remains of fallen trees, and the unpredictable drumbeat of a woodpecker at work echoed across the landscape. While I didn't encounter the elk, which left piles of scat along the trail, I did spy mule deer grazing in the distance.

The land had been restored. Fire had removed dense shrubs and brush, allowing sun and rain to reach the lowest parts of the forest, the understory. Invasive species, like leafy spurge, had been cleared from the forest floor. With the help of rain, nutrients had trickled into the soil, reviving it. Bacteria, fungi, nematodes, and earthworms—the living components of soil—would soon follow. The heat from the fire had also melted the pine cones of the loblolly pine, a tree whose cones only open when exposed to fire. For many other seeds, heat had given life a little nudge and triggered them to sprout. Seedlings filled the open spaces, creating a home for insects, reptiles, birds, and mammals. Within weeks of the prescribed burn, new connections strengthened the forest's network of complex relationships, healing the land.

Prescribed burns also eliminated fuel for wildfires. If not managed, dense stands of midsized ponderosa pines will form fire ladders, pathways for flames. As wildfire climbs into the treetops, it burns out of control at extremely high temperatures. Removing the younger trees had reduced the risk of wildfire in the Lolo National Forest.

As I learned on the hike, fire is an essential part of life in what are known as fire-dependent ecosystems. Fire suppression, a long-held practice, actually leaves land more vulnerable to wild-fire. During my time in Montana, my lifelong fear of fire had transformed into a new understanding: fire can be a natural reset button, an opportunity for new things to take hold.

Eight years ago, I moved to Central Texas and settled on a piece of overgrazed ranchland. Covered in dry, hay-like silver bluestem (a grass used for cattle feed), a tangled mess of dewberry vines, an ever-expanding patch of prickly pear cactus, and a few scrubby trees, mostly thorny huisache and persimmon, the view was anything but stunning. Over time wind had eroded the soil, leaving behind a crumbling expanse of limestone, visible at the base of the blades of grass. At first glance, the land resembled an abandoned lot or a neglected roadside.

Unlike my neighbors, who were content to mow down the grasses, I envisioned a natural landscape, one where roadrunners, walking sticks, damsel flies, moths, and bees would roam. As a biologist, finding home in a new place comes from meeting all the neighbors, including the ones with wings and tails and rows of legs. Knowing a place comes from a deep understanding of the land—its geology, ecology, and history. As a science writer, joy comes from sharing those stories.

After some initial research, I learned that my new home is part of the savanna ecoregion, a place where bison, wolves, and bear once wandered, according to early German settlers and natural-ists. A savanna is a grassland ecosystem similar to a prairie, but, unlike in a prairie, trees also thrive in the landscape. Here live oak and Ashe juniper are the dominant tree species.

Where I live is also one of the top ten fastest-growing counties in the country. Day by day, urban sprawl devours the rural land-scape. When human populations rise, development follows and prairies disappear, giving them the title of the most threatened ecosystem in North America. As with ranching and farming, development leaves prairies fragmented and broken, in need of healing.

With this in mind, I began a long-term restoration experiment. My goal was to re-create and nurture a native habitat known as a pocket prairie, a prairie of less than one acre. (Technically my yard is a pocket savanna, but it is referred to as a prairie more often in the literature.) With the help of my husband, I sprinkled native grass and wildflower seeds. I walked over the seeds, pressing them into the ground and covering them with a thin blanket of soil. Belowground, the long roots of the grasses will prevent soil erosion and help filter and store water. Aboveground, the grasses will provide food (seed) and shelter for animals. Other than the path we mowed, the backyard required minimal maintenance.

A few weeks after we found the rough green snake, a loud *thunk* rattles the windows along the back of my house. I head to the family room, afraid of what I might find. A dead bird is lying on the porch. Despite the bird's horrifying and untimely demise, I can't stop staring. The bird has an unusually long, black tail with half-dollar-sized white spots. Similar in size to a crow, it has cinnamon-colored wings and a mustard-yellow beak. I have never seen anything like it.

After failing to identify the bird using field guides, I open Merlin, Cornell University's bird app. I type a few characteristics into the search box and a video pops up. Again I find myself staring, mesmerized by the secretive yellow-billed cuckoo. The cuckoo's call is a haunting rattle—*ka-ka-ka-kow-kow-kolp*—arising from deep in the bird's belly. I recognize the sound right away. I have heard it in my backyard, but I assumed it was a frog. Some mornings the cuckoos' calls were so loud, they drowned out the other music of the prairie. Naturalists refer to cuckoos as rain crows or storm crows because, like frogs, they greet storms with song, a trait I admire.

The next day a research group tags the cuckoo photo I posted on iNaturalist. I click on the tab to reveal more information: yellow-billed cuckoo populations are in decline because they rely on tall grasses for survival. Other species I have discovered living in our yard are also in decline, like fireflies, which breed in the tall grasses, and rainbow-colored painted buntings, birds whose diet consists of native grass seeds.

I start to wonder if my pocket prairie is more than a hobby. Could it be a valuable habitat for species not found in neighboring yards? Or, as I worry from time to time, is my backyard an over-grown field of weeds, a breeding ground for venomous snakes, or, even more disturbing, a fire hazard?

Ryland, his strawberry-blond hair catching the wind like wings, flies down the steepest hill in our neighborhood on his scooter. He hoots and hollers all the way to the bottom, not a surprise since he has been cooped up in the house all day. As spring turns to summer, we have been sheltering in place for more than two months, a result of the COVID-19 pandemic. Because temperatures soar into the upper nineties during the day, the evening is one of the only times I dare to set foot outside.

After trying unsuccessfully to slow himself down by dragging the toe of his shoe on the pavement, Ryland jumps, arms flailing, leaving the scooter to veer off and crash into the tall grasses by the side of the road. Trailing behind, I stop and rescue the scooter from the ditch. I realize I am standing at the far edge of my neighbor's yard, the same neighbor who had set his yard on fire the year before. Because his property is not on my usual route through the neighborhood, I haven't given it much thought since then.

Now, standing on the outskirts of my neighbor's property, I wonder if he, like the Forest Service crew in Montana, had performed a prescribed burn. Grasslands, like Montana forests, are fire-dependent ecosystems. The benefits of burning prairies include the elimination of thatch (dead grass material) and the removal of invasive species.

While native species have adapted to fire, invasive species found in grasslands do not stand a chance. My mind drifts to the stubborn thorny huisache, prickly pear cactus, and johnsongrass that threaten to take over my backyard and choke out other species. If left alone, a stand of huisache saplings would tower over my head within a few years. The limbs and leaves would form a dense canopy, blocking the sunlight required for grasses and wildflowers to flourish. I have to admit, a prescribed burn would solve multiple problems in my backyard.

The next day I decide to contact my neighbor. With the curtains drawn and the garage door closed, his house shows no signs of life. The less-than-welcoming appearance convinces me to stick a note in the mailbox. Written on my special occasion stationery—an American bumblebee on the front with the Latin name, *Bombus pensylvanicus*, below the picture—I explain that I am a pocket prairie enthusiast and am curious if he shares my interests. I include my contact information.

On the walk home, I imagine the two of us unfolding our lawn chairs and sitting down to share a beer in the tall grasses. We would discuss prescribed burns, wildflower diversity, and other prairie-related issues the way other neighbors lean over their fences and chat about tomato plants. Did he notice more flowers, more insects, more birds than before? How did he prevent the flames from spreading? I have endless questions.

In the meantime, I call the county fire marshal's office. I leave a message asking if prescribed burns are allowed, and the next day I receive a brief voicemail in response. Not sure that I have understood correctly, I call back with a follow-up question. I decide to be direct: "I own one acre off of Farm-to-Market Road 306. Can I perform a prescribed burn on my property, which is located in a residential neighborhood?" The assistant fire marshal tells me that as long as there isn't a burn ban in effect (a regulation that prohibits outdoor burning during periods of drought) and I live outside the city limits, which I do, I can set my yard on fire.

Out of disbelief, I blurt out one last question. "It isn't illegal to light my yard on fire?" I say. In an impatient voice, the assistant fire marshal assures me, for the third time, that it is no problem.

Although I recognize the beneficial role of fire in prairie ecosystems, I decide I am not willing to accept the risk. I have not been trained to perform prescribed burns. In Montana, I learned about the weeks leading up to a burn and the enormous amount of planning involved—the maps, the trenches, the timing, and the wind and weather considerations. I also learned about wildfires.

I arrive at the Lady Bird Johnson Wildflower Center, a research site for the University of Texas in Austin, to investigate the use of mowing as a tool for prairie maintenance. While I am not ready to light my yard on fire, mowing is a reasonable alternative.

Ryland and I fiddle with our surgical masks before we leave the car. At ten a.m. on a July morning, it is already ninety-five degrees. The usually crowded parking lot is nearly empty, a result of the pandemic. A clever sign, complete with drawings, reminds us to wear our masks and stay five roadrunners apart from other groups.

Past the parking lot, the visitors' pavilion is barricaded behind plexiglass, rope, and neon-orange cones. Jumping up and down, Ryland waves the paper with our reservation confirmation, and an older woman sends us through the entrance. Seven hundred acres open up before us.

Although the center is fifty miles north of my home, the biology and geology are similar. Both places are located within the Edwards Aquifer recharge zone, an area where the aquifer, a subterranean water source, lies just beneath the surface. And both sit atop the limestone ledges of the Edwards Plateau.

For twenty years, scientists and volunteers at the center have conducted research on the ecology of prairie ecosystems. They eagerly share their findings with the public because, in Texas, 96 percent of land is privately owned. When it comes to grassland conservation, landowners play a critical role.

From the Simmons Research Trail, Ryland and I view the project's results. The study plots occupy seventy acres of land. Some of the plots have been burned, others have been mowed, and the control plots have been left alone. The frequency of the treatment (mow or burn), as well as the season, varies. Some plots are mowed at the beginning of every season, while others are only mowed in the summer. Metal signs, sticking out of the tall grasses, let us know which treatment has taken place.

I tell Ryland that we are making a list of what we see, the more the better. As I have learned over the past few years, the secret of the prairies extends beyond the plants themselves to include the community of creatures living in and around the grasses. On the mown plots, do we see the same wildflowers as we see at home? Are there more beetles or grasshoppers? Is there a variety of grasses? Biodiversity is a strong indicator of prairie health.

I let Ryland take the lead. Following his favorite color, yellow, he counts butterflies in the first meadow: little yellows, yellow sulfurs, and his favorite species, the black swallowtail, with its lightning-colored dots. We also note the sea of saffron-yellow petals with black centers—black-eyed Susans—a wildflower that has exploded in our yard too, because of the timing of the spring rains.

Next, in a field of dry, golden grasses, a different color distracts Ryland from his yellow-themed quest. He points to a red cardinal, but the crumpled crease at the corner of his mouth suggests he is not impressed with this bird. "I like chickadees better because I speak three languages: English, Spanish, and Chickadee," he says. To demonstrate, he inhales and puffs out his chest, releasing a piercing rendition of the bird's call: *chicka-dee-dee-dee.* If there were any other birds in the area, they are gone now.

Soon a pair of firecracker-red neon skimmers zoom over our heads. Like all dragonflies, they are expert fliers. The pair dip and dart like high-speed synchronized swimmers, never leaving one another's side. Ryland and I continue hiking and adding to our list in a zigzagging, entirely unscientific way. As usual, the company of a little boy overshadows the science.

As we walk, we make plans for our pocket prairie. Ryland wants a pond to attract more dragonflies. I suspect he senses something familiar about that species.

Ahead, two college-aged women carrying nets emerge from the grasses. They quickly pull up their masks and step off the crushed granite path to avoid us. I can't help but ask, "Collecting insects today?" Prior to the pandemic, I visited the center every Thursday to work on the Fauna Project. As a Master Naturalist volunteer, I collected data on insects and other animals that rely on wildflower habitat. It would have been fun to let the young women show Ryland how to use the nets or hear about their most unusual finds of the day. Maybe, tucked into glass vials in their backpacks, they had collected something spectacular for Ryland to observe. But the women nod and move on.

Ryland and I agree that the mown plots appear similar to our pocket prairie. Mowing should help to control some of the invasive species, like johnsongrass, and decrease thatch buildup too. But just to be sure, a few days after our visit, I get in touch with Sean Griffin, a postdoctoral fellow at the University of Texas. He has been analyzing data from the center's study plots for the past year.

I ask Griffin what he thinks are the best management practices for a backyard pocket prairie like mine. He recommends mowing every two to three years in the late summer or early fall. Doing so in a rotating mosaic pattern, where some patches of tall grass remain for food and shelter, is an even better idea. To prevent thatch buildup, he suggests raking and mentions that deer grazing is effective too. (We have that covered, I assure him.) He also encourages me to continue removing invasive species and woody growth by hand.

According to Griffin, I should focus on increasing the number of forbs (wildflowers), something that happens naturally when one mows, which spreads seeds and opens up space. Because it is a small-scale restoration project, increasing wildflower density and diversity is where my backyard can have the greatest impact in terms of conservation, especially for pollinator species and other beneficial insects.

As an example, Griffin mentions the American bumblebee, the one on my stationery, and the same fuzzy species that swarms the Texas sage shrub near the window in front of my writing desk. Around Austin, American bumblebee populations are declining, a result of habitat loss. What we plant in our backyards, even the smallest yards, can have an impact, Griffin points out. During our conversations his exuberance for pollinators and forbs overflows, and he offers to visit and prepare a presentation for my neighbors. (I don't have the heart to tell him I would have trouble finding an audience.) Perhaps best of all, Griffin explains that pocket prairies are too small to provide the appropriate habitat for venomous snakes. Phew.

Like a secret, a prairie's complexity lies hidden in plain sight. What is often mistaken for a field of weeds—an unkept and forgotten place—becomes home to a multitude of plants and animals. If you pay attention, the secrets will reveal themselves in unexpected ways, in the form of the black-and-white spotted tail of a yellow-billed cuckoo or the shimmering scales of a rough green snake.

I never did hear back from my neighbor who burned his yard last year. I wonder if he knows about the relationships that develop and thrive in the tall grasses; I wonder if he knows a disturbance, like a fire or a virus, can lead to healing.

NAVIGATING
ROCKY TERRAIN

. . . a landscape untouched by disturbance would lack complexity and completeness.
— TOM WESSELS, PROFESSOR OF ECOLOGY

I focus on my feet. The rocky surface is smooth, the incline steep. The climb up Summit Trail, equivalent to ascending a thirty-story building, offers the most direct route up the face of Enchanted Rock. My teenage sons take off by leaps and bounds, my husband not far behind. Ryland considers every step, something out of character. He holds my hand, but pulls back, as if he expects me to drag him uphill. At the same time, my muscles tug at my bones. I try inhaling, long and deep, but my lungs demand more, so I resort to shallow, frequent breaths. When I pause to take in the view, I feel dizzy, off-balance. My eyes dart back to my feet. Almost immediately, I reconsider, certain an easier path exists.

I coax Ryland along, but halfway up the mountain, he freezes. He feels like he is falling. I don't push. I remember trips to Cadillac Mountain in Maine. Every summer, my family joined throngs of tourists scrambling over the flat, expansive summit near our family cabin. Accidents were rare, and despite thick ropes placed in precarious places, my eyes read the landscape as one gigantic edge. Every time, I felt like I was falling.

Ryland's teenage brothers swoop in and surround him. They offer to finish the hike like this—one above and one below. A human safety net. Ryland agrees reluctantly. We continue climbing, slow and steady.

TWO YEARS AGO

My father's call awakened me long before sunrise on a spring morning, a few days after Mother's Day. With his soft voice barely recognizable, the story flowed in a stream of choppy, high-pitched phrases, as if he couldn't find enough air to breathe. This is what I gathered: my mother had suffered a stroke. She had awakened, complained of a severe headache, and then, within minutes, she was gone. In time, I would be thankful that a stroke had ended her long struggle with dementia, but not in that moment.

I listened from far away, a cold, plastic phone case pressed against my ear, while my father sat alone in the hospital hallway, wondering what to do, where to go. He had left home in the ambulance without his cane; he would leave the hospital without his wife. They had been lifelong partners, married for more than forty years. How do you stand up and walk back out into the world after something like that?

A few months later, my father carried a black box filled with my mother's ashes to our family cabin in Maine and placed the box on top of the kitchen cabinets, near his favorite chair. It was already there when I arrived. Why had my father picked that spot, and how had he managed to get the heavy box up so high?

Cremation was something my mother had mentioned more than once. It made sense: where else would she be, but with us? She belonged to the bay. We all did. But her ashes up there make me anxious. When will we send them off? Who will do it? Who is going to be there? There seems to be no plan, at least not one that has been discussed.

I avoid looking at my mother's box on the cabinet. I imagine what's inside—a thick, generic plastic bag, impossibly heavy, nothing like my mother. I don't let myself think about what her body endured. After the stroke, my father kept her on life support until I arrived. My mother was waiting for me at the hospital. I was afraid of her lifeless body, and so I didn't go. Now our last moments together would come down to a box, as if a box could hold all that was. I miss my mother's soft skin, the clinking of her bracelets. If I could do it over, I would hold her hand and let her go. At least, that is what I envision, but I am not that brave.

As the sun sets, Bryant opens the bag and lets my mother's ashes drift out with the tide. The boys are watching TV because I don't want to see the sadness on their faces. I don't want them to see me cry—a loud, choking, awful cry that might not end. Instead, I want them to hold on to the image of my mother walking with them on the beach and searching for sea glass. My father, his legs too unsteady to carry him to the water's edge, sits on a rock, the one with the remnants of a rusty anchor.

The next day, my father calls the Neptune Society. He makes arrangements with the Scattering Services Department, a name I can barely fathom. He picks out the Sea Package, the same package his father had purchased years before. As part of the deal, a stranger will toss my father's ashes somewhere in the ocean off the California coast.

I don't speak, but my face conveys confusion: I had assumed I would scatter my father's ashes in the bay, to be with my mother. This new plan will be easier for me, my father states and checks another thing off his lengthy, end-of-life to-do list. Although my father was born in California, for me, the business-like arrangement feels wrong—too practical, too detached, too lonely—but I nod, unable to argue. I am his only child, and I have just lost my mother. To enter into that conversation would mean accepting that he, too, will be missing from my life, another enormous, gaping hole.

A curious conversation led me to this place, hiking toward the summit of Enchanted Rock.

"You haven't been to Enchanted Rock?" a local plant guru had inquired several weeks earlier, astonishment evident in her voice. "There are plants growing there you won't find anywhere else." As she told me more about Enchanted Rock, she mapped out a pollinator garden near a new water feature in my yard. I jumped at the opportunity to hear about something unusual, somewhere new to explore.

Geologically speaking, Enchanted Rock is a batholith, although it is commonly referred to as a mountain. It shares a similar geological history with El Capitan in Yosemite National Park and Stone Mountain in Georgia. Born miles underground from a pocket of molten rock, Enchanted Rock slowly turned to granite as the magma cooled and crystalized deep in the Earth's crust. Then, as tectonic plates shifted and collided, the immense pressure uplifted the granite until it broke through the limestone surface, shattering rock into pieces.

When compared with Montana's Bitterroot Mountains, Colorado's Rocky Mountains, or even Cadillac Mountain, Enchanted Rock is a mere bump. It rises 425 feet above the surrounding plain and, along with several other smaller peaks, covers 640 acres. The majority of the pear-shaped mountain still exists belowground, hidden from sight. Near Fredericksburg, Texas, the sunset-red rock stands out against the flat, limestone landscape like a granite beacon.

According to myths, the mountain creaks and moans, giving it the lesser known name of Crying Rock. Although scientists explain the phenomenon as something that happens when rock heats up and expands, and then cools and contracts, many still believe the noises are the spirit voices of their ancestors roaming the land. I listen, but only hear the slight sound of my feet as they fall into a familiar rhythm. From somewhere within, my body recognizes the granite, something like muscle memory or perhaps something deeper.

In his book *The Granite Landscape: A Natural History of America's Mountain Domes, from Acadia to Yosemite*, Tom Wessels compares the harsh growing conditions and perpetual disturbances characteristic of granite domes and explains that "someone who grew up on Mount Desert Island, Maine, would feel very much at home atop Yosemite's lofty domes." Perhaps this is the reason why, for me, a granite dome in Texas, so far from Maine, can feel like home. I think of my father often as I climb, how he, too, would have felt curious about this unusual and out-of-place mountain.

Not far from the summit of Enchanted Rock, lichen appear underfoot, giving the granite a tie-dye pattern. I step over the waves of color spreading across the rocky surface, a habit formed in childhood. The composite organisms, symbiotic relationships between algae and fungi, are the first signs of life on the rocks. Like the lichens on Maine mountaintops, some are grayish-white and sea green and others a golden color. Lichen species grow on particular surfaces—some on tree bark, some on soil, some on limestone, and some on granite. They release an acid that weakens rock, especially along cracks and broken places. Then thread-like filaments creep farther into the layers, chipping away flecks of rock. Eventually a fine soil develops—an environment perfect for plants to take root and new life to begin.

Still, it is not an easy life. Exposed, mountaintop species are vulnerable to high winds, swift runoff, intense heat, rapid evaporation, and extended drought. In order to adapt to the harsh conditions and natural disturbances, lichen go dormant. Their colors fade, and they transition into a crumbling dust, like ash. Then they wait for a clue that it is safe, that it is time to reawaken. Following a rainfall, they spring back to life, photosynthesizing and reproducing rapidly. This lifestyle is the ultimate example of adaptation to disturbance—of patience, persistence, and resilience. I take photographs, as reminders.

When I was a little girl, I played a game on the rocks near our family cabin. The challenge: to avoid touching the ground, or in my imagination, the abyss—some dark, unknowable place far below. Scanning the rocky shore, I calculated my every move. Perched on a blue-gray rock the shape of an artist's palette, I stretched my leg until I could almost touch another rock with my tippy toes, and then I leapt. Balance was key. The next rock resembled a desk, complete with a wedge-like seat. Its coarse surface warmed the bottoms of my feet, and the wind carried the scent of sunbaked seaweed. Next I jumped to a loaf of bread, balancing on the cracked dome of a knee-high, chocolate-brown boulder. Round and round, from rock to rock, I memorized a path through the rubble.

One day my father interrupted my game. I looked up, surprised by the crunch of footsteps sinking into the pebbly sand. He had returned from the hardware store and decided to take a short break from his latest project. The dilapidated A-frame came with a lifelong to-do list, and, for my father, vacation was not a time for rest.

As he made his way down the beach, my father stopped now and then, bent down, and scooped something up. When he reached my side, he held out his hands, where several granite rocks rested on his palms. He shared their stories: something about quartz and feldspar and wavy layers of green chlorite. For me, the geological details sailed through the air, carried away by an invisible breeze. Before long, I left my father's side.

My father was a collector, not only of rocks, but of facts and stories and memories. He scribbled notes and ideas and questions on pocket-sized pads of paper, always on hand. He loved old cars and model airplanes and war stories and physics. Sometimes I sat with my grandfather and my father and listened to stories about World War II, about my great-grandfather's early career on a medicine wagon, about the Oregon Trail, and about people who were long gone . . . but only because it was expected. Side by side, the two men never spoke of how the war had fractured their family.

Weeks later, as we closed the cabin for the season, my father carried jam jars full of rocks to the car. Back home, he shared the rocks with his youngest psychiatric patients, whom he guided through their own fractured lives. He told them stories about the rocks, too—the special places they came from and why they sparkled, even though they had been tossed and toppled by the waves. He placed the jars in between piles of towels, for safekeeping.

On the summit of Enchanted Rock, lichen activity and water erosion form granite depressions, like terrestrial tide pools. I stop to examine the pits or depression communities, hoping to find something unusual. There are more than one hundred of these formations, ranging in size from one foot up to fifty feet long, each one a unique microhabitat. Some of the smaller pits hold water. Some of the larger pits house a significant amount of soil and look like mini-prairies with tall grasses. Fairy shrimp and rock quillwort, an ancient, spore-producing, grasslike plant, are reported to be some of the unusual residents.

So resilient are these stress-adapted species that scientists come to study life in the pits. They survey the summit in search of plants that can survive in extreme conditions. These plants are selected for use in green roof projects across the country. I envy their ability to start over and over again.

The landscape reminds me of one of my father's favorite spots: Schoodic Point, not far from our cabin. There the rocky ledges tell a tumultuous tale, one I heard over and over again. Intersecting dikes of basalt and other crystalline rock cut through the granite, creating a stone mosaic. Similar to Enchanted Rock, the granite is salmon pink, a result of high concentrations of feldspar crystals.

During one of our visits, my father meandered over ledges and fed seagulls, throwing squishy white bread high above his head and watching the birds swoop down to catch it in their beaks. I tried to throw pieces of bread as high as my father. Later my parents sat together along the cliff's edge, legs dangling. Waves crashed against the granite with a boom and showered them with salty droplets. I worried that they were too close to the edge.

The visit ended with a search for tide pools, the best around. My mother and I crouched down alongside a depression no bigger than a puddle. Habitats like that had been carved out by the pounding waves. Copepods, small shrimp-like crustaceans, darted across the pool when I reached in and lifted a flat rock. I plucked a periwinkle, waited for its slimy foot to emerge, and stuck the snail to my skin.

I never knew what I would find, as everything changed from tide to tide within those temporary worlds.

ONE YEAR AGO

My phone rang midmorning, not in the middle of the night or some other odd hour, so there was no reason to be alarmed at first. With a shaky voice, my oldest son told me the police had just contacted him. I needed to call my father right away; something was wrong. Panic hit with such intensity, like a landslide.

When I called my father, an unfamiliar voice answered. My father had collapsed near the elevator in his apartment building, according to the police officer. Emergency responders had been trying CPR for twenty minutes with no response. I ran to the other room and shoved the phone into my husband's hands, thinking somehow, he might change the outcome. After a short exchange, my husband hung up the phone, shook his head. My father was gone.

We were told to stay home, to stay safe, to avoid catching COVID-19, but I had no choice. The next day Bryant, Ryland, and I flew from Texas to Virginia to sort through my father's belongings, empty the refrigerator, find a home for Elmer, the cat. A whirlwind of activity. I couldn't find the paperwork for the Sea Package, so I would have to make a new plan for my father.

The following week, a box marked "Priority Mail Express" arrived at my door. I had known the box was coming, but still, I was unprepared, lost in the suddenness of it all. I longed to ask my father what to do.

Through a blur of tears, I held out my hands and received the box from a stranger. I signed my name, shut the door, and sank to the floor. A weight pressed down on me, the great responsibility I held, alone: the safekeeping of my father's body.

Even as I closed my eyes, the words, written on fluorescent orange tape, flashed across the darkness: CREMATED REMAINS. I sat there, hugging the box close to my chest and wondering: *how could this be?*

It was July. My father and I were supposed to be together at our family cabin, just like we had been every July for as long as I could remember. But vacationing during a pandemic had been too risky, so we stayed home, isolated from one another during the last weeks of my father's life.

When I finally gathered myself, I stood up from the floor and walked to my closet. I laid my father's box in between the Christmas tree skirt and my winter sweaters. And then I waited . . . for what I wasn't sure.

As the pandemic dragged on, having my father's box nearby became a comfort. I talked with him in the morning as I started my day and every night before bed. I asked questions and listened for answers. From silence, I attempted to conjure my father's stories, even the boring ones about geology. But, as time passed, the arrangement felt more like a selfish act and less like a comfort.

After making our way down from the summit, my family explores near the base of Enchanted Rock, a landscape frozen in time. Boulders appear to have paused mid-roll, balancing on ledges up and down the mountainside, as if a landslide ceased suddenly. At ground level, rock fragments cover the ground in different stages of disintegration, from boulders the size of compact cars or basketballs, to pebbles and sandy soil. My sons jump from rock to rock and I follow; I know this game well. The boys scramble up larger boulders, trying to find their way through the erratic landscape.

Looking back up at Enchanted Rock, I see cracked sheets of curved rock, like a broken puzzle, cleave off the sloped sides. Over time, they will come crashing down, revealing a smooth, rounded dome beneath. A billion years ago, the granite pushed upward through layers of limestone. As the soil and limestone that overlaid the granite eroded, the granite crystals expanded due to a decrease in pressure. Water also entered into the smallest fractured areas and expanded when temperatures dropped. Rock layers, like those of an onion, began to crack and peel away. This process, much like shedding skin, is called exfoliation. As it has done for millions of years, Enchanted Rock continued to crumble and shift, something similar to aging.

This is the rock cycle, up close and personal. I try to comprehend how something so solid, so impenetrable, can crumble, almost as easily as a human life.

Several weeks after my first visit to Enchanted Rock, I pull out a crumpled rock-climbing map from the bottom of my backpack. Dotted lines indicate routes with captivating names like Edge of

Night, Fear of Flying, Dungeon, and Lichen Delight. Some of the routes reveal places to boulder, a type of free climbing that doesn't require ropes or harnesses. Because I am afraid of heights and edges, these routes have been invisible to me.

When I was in college, I volunteered on the trail crew at Acadia National Park on Mount Desert Island, Maine, close to our family cabin. There I learned the intricacies of reading a landscape: how to identify the best slope for setting a staircase, or how to create a stable log crossing along the edges of a bog, or how to wind a trail through a series of diverse ecosystems. Like stories, trails introduce people to places and guide them through unfamiliar territory.

In the same way that I had learned to read the land, I imagine rock climbers develop a unique intimacy with rock, as they envision pathways up rock faces. It turns out that the most common way to develop a new route is to follow a crack in the rock, an approach known as crack climbing. In order to locate and communicate about handholds and footholds, crack systems are described by width: finger cracks, hand cracks, and chimney cracks, for example. At first the route is not easily seen, but by studying the rock and understanding all of the cracks and crevices and broken places, climbers find a way up and over. And from there, the world is seen anew.

I think more and more about pathways through rocky terrain, how I have been practicing since childhood with my parents close by, how that skill might help me to navigate the world without them. The challenge is to find a foothold in the cracks . . . and then climb up.

Days later, something nudges me from within. Like the lichen, I am ready to step out of my self-imposed dormancy. I unearth my father's box from layers of sweaters. I tear away tape and cardboard and gently lift out the inner box. I remove the plastic bag, cut a small opening, and pour a handful of my father's ashes into a container, saving the rest for our return to Maine.

* * *

On my second visit to Enchanted Rock, I arrive with a different purpose; the long-awaited decision has been made. I feel both relief and urgency, a signal to my father that, after an entire year, he hasn't been tucked away and forgotten. Even though my husband reminds me often that a body is just a temporary container, I need to send my father on his way. He had never been one to sit around and wait for things to happen, and so, I am sure he has things to do.

Bryant and I start off down a forested trail. At the last minute, I decided the boys should stay home. I wanted to make it easier on them. Like when Bryant scattered my mother's ashes, I didn't want them to see me cry—a loud, choking, awful cry that might not end.

The first time I saw my father cry, my uncle was sick with cancer. I had been afraid to look at my father's face, and so I distracted myself with all the other details: his white hair, his dry and sagging skin, his worn loafers. The details had seemed all wrong; that was not my father. Never before had I comforted him, and I had no idea how to reach out. We rarely hugged, even when I was a child, and so I stood across the table—a space that felt as enormous as a gorge—witnessing the layers of my father's hardened exterior slip away.

We come to a clearing and Bryant points to three massive, lichen-covered boulders, almost as tall as the trees. They lean on one another, off-kilter, the way families do. Wildflowers peek out from the cracks and crevices. My father would have pointed things out, too, things I would have missed, like the dust-covered rocks at our feet. Without the cooperation of his arthritic knees, he would ask me to lean down and scoop them up, and then, after naming them, he would pass the pebbles to me for safekeeping.

Standing in the clearing, the spot feels right. My father will feel at home, nestled near the granite mountains, surrounded by rocks of all shapes and sizes, with his family close by. Because I hesitate, Bryant kneels and mixes a handful of my father's ashes with the granite soil, near daisy-like flowers, called *Helenium amarum.* The bumblebee yellow color of their petals symbolizes enlightenment, remembrance, intellect, honor, loyalty, and joy.

Bryant and I fall silent as we meander back over granite outcrops, up and over the rolling terrain. Footprints, both coming and going, overlap on the dusty trail. With hushed voices, we plan our next visit to Enchanted Rock. I feel at peace, knowing that a part of my father will be at home here, and that he is nearby. The rest of his ashes will be with my mother in Maine. I hadn't followed father's wishes, to let a stranger sprinkle his ashes in California, but saying goodbye was never going to be easy for me, something my father had failed to realize—something I had failed to express.

THROUGH
THE LAYERS

The only way to explore the depths of Canyon Lake Gorge is with a guide. It is a protected place, under the care of the Gorge Preservation Society and the Guadalupe-Blanco River Authority. A few years ago, my youngest son, Ryland, wasn't old enough to join a tour group, so I visited on my own. But today he is eight years old and ready for the hike. It feels like a geological rite of passage, a time for him to learn about the vulnerable, rock-covered place he comes from.

As we head out the door, Ryland tightens the Velcro straps on his Minecraft sneakers and throws his matching hoodie, with emerald and lime-green blocks, into the backseat. He reminds me that a Minecraft mod recently released the Caves & Cliffs Update. He has been digging virtual holes and exploring virtual tunnels for weeks. I am thankful that today we will plunge our hands in dirt and clay, the kind that requires tons of bubbles to wash away.

During the fifteen-minute drive from our house, we talk about one of my favorite topics: holes and cracks. Where we live in Central Texas, holes, cracks, and crevices are common landscape features. Our family moved here from Houston while I was pregnant. Unlike his two older brothers, Ryland was born here.

Ryland's voice rises and he wiggles in his seat, as he tells me about how, last year, he and his friends dug holes while waiting in the pickup line at the elementary school. No easy feat because, after removing an inch or less of soil, they hit rock. Ever optimistic, Ryland chipped away at the rocky layer, day after day, in search of fossils. "We should do that again," he adds, as he stares out the window.

Soon conversation turns to one of Ryland's favorite games: Would You Rather. He tosses out a good one to start, "Would you rather be a mythological beast or a superhero?" We both choose mythological beasts, and so we begin our early morning adventure together, the mermaid and the centaur.

EXPOSED LAYERS

After a short shuttle ride, our tour group gathers near the top of the rolled earth dam, an enormous grass-covered barrier. Hailey, our guide, is running her first solo tour because her training partner called in sick. She chatters to fill the silences. The group, a family with two teenagers, a father and young son, two friends, Ryland, and myself, sit on benches.

Hailey tells the story of how the gorge was born. Eighteen years ago, after a week of heavy rainfall and historic flooding, a seven-foot surge of water crashed over the concrete barrier of Canyon Lake Dam, just north of San Antonio, Texas. Floodwaters rushed over the dam's spillway for six weeks straight, overflowing the banks of the Guadalupe River on its journey to the Gulf Coast. After the water receded, layers of eroded Cretaceous rock lay at the surface. Hailey holds laminated maps and photos as the wind whips them around. We view the before and after—a juniper-covered landscape erased, replaced by bare rock.

It was as if Earth's flesh had been peeled away, exposing bone or perhaps something deeper.

Hailey was a toddler, not much older than my oldest son, at the time of the flood. This is her first job after college graduation and her new-job enthusiasm is contagious. "I never thought I'd be talking about science so much," she exclaims as we head down the trail. I look forward to experiencing this place through her eyes.

Canyon Lake Gorge extends for a mile before us, like an enormous window to the past, revealing a subterranean world rarely seen. If the flood had not been witnessed, this place could be easily mistaken for a deep, dry riverbed. Staring up from a narrow ravine at the face of a jagged rock wall forty feet tall, it's as if the rushing water carved an image of itself in stone, with endless layers, undulating like waves frozen in time.

Geologists separate these rocks into layers and formations (or units) based on similar physical characteristics such as color, texture, strength, and size. All of these characteristics are a result of environmental conditions like temperature, pressure, and depth. Given the right conditions, rock melts, collides, collapses, folds, intrudes, and morphs into something altogether different, something akin to geological shapeshifting.

Pausing near a watermelon-sized boulder that resembles Swiss cheese, Hailey poses a question, "How did these holes get here?" When no one responds, she cries out "Worms!" Ryland's eyes widen. He sticks his pointer finger into a hole bigger than a half dollar and whispers, "Those must have been big worms."

Hailey pours water over the top of the boulder. We watch as the water trickles out of the holes, called vugs, on all sides. It reminds me of one of Ryland's old bathtub toys. The holes that were first carved by worms have been enlarged by the flow of water. These limestone rocks are described as porous and permeable, or vuggy, meaning water travels freely in, under, around, through, and between interconnected pathways in the rock layers.

Throughout the gorge, limestone exists in varying shades of white, cream, gray, and sandy brown. Some of the thin, exposed layers are soft and crumbly, prone to dissolution from rainwater; other layers are thick, solid, and more resistant. Each layer, like a family, relies on the older rock below as it forms, building upward.

Each unique limestone formation, representing a specific time period, receives a name. The rocks at the gorge are part of the Glen Rose Formation, a layer consisting of limestone, siltstone, clay, and dolomite, a limestone-type crystalline rock. They make up a subunit of the Trinity Group, a rock type that extends throughout Texas, Arkansas, Mississippi, New Mexico, and Oklahoma.

Move in any direction, and the characteristics of the rock might change and receive a different name, similar to the way mushrooms or fish carry a taste of place, depending on the soil, sea of origin, or local food source. Together the porous limestone layers and their features, like caves, springs, disappearing streams, and sinkholes, are called karst.

Haley informs us that the karst layers at the bottom of the gorge are particularly fossiliferous, meaning they contain an abundance of fossils. She stumbles over the word several times before she gets it out. Laughing, Ryland and I try to say fossiliferous as fast as we can, like a tongue twister. I hope he will always share my love of stories and languages and sounds.

Our group stops to investigate a crumbling limestone wall. Hailey pulls out laminated pages from her backpack and lays them on the ground. They serve as a field guide with pictures and the names of fossils we may find hidden in the layers: several snail species, worm tubes, sea urchins, and clam-like bivalves. Given a challenge, Ryland and the other young boy form a team and get to work. Their voices rise with excitement. "Look at this one!" "Over here!" "I found another one!" Soon piles encircle the laminated pages. I sit close by, journal in hand, listening for stories.

Deeper beneath the gorge, out of reach of the floodwaters, other karst stories are buried in the layers: stories of ancient seas that formed, then receded, and then formed again, submerging and exposing rock over billions of years. There are other water stories, too, at the surface: stories of rivers that pushed and squeezed and carved through the limestone, leaving behind a terrain of hills and canyons. This is how, layer by layer, the area of Central Texas, known as the Hill Country, was born.

CRACKED LAYERS

Faults create change. They leave behind disturbed places where nothing is ever the same. My home and Canyon Lake Gorge lie within the Balcones Fault Zone, a large swath of land that runs from southwest to north-central Texas, like a comma. Looking at a geological map, the faults, represented by red squiggles, cover the surface like a choppy, red sea. Geologists are unsure whether the thousands of faults, both big and small, formed all at once or over a long period of time.

In my own life, the pattern is familiar: beginnings and endings, stops and starts, shifts—marriage, new jobs, leaving New England for Texas, travel, motherhood, an unexpected baby at forty, going back to school, a series of lost loved ones. In the past two years, the COVID-19 pandemic and historic Winter Storm Uri, the "snowpocalypse," have left me with the unsettling feeling that life has been interrupted, on hold for far too long. I imagine these events like red squiggles on the map of my body, reaching below the surface and through the layers.

Lately I have had the inexplicable urge to stare into the depths of a fault. Faults are the reason for my visit to Canyon Lake Gorge on this early September morning. According to the gorge website, visible faults are scattered throughout the gorge.

I want to press my hand against the uneven layers and cracks that run like scars on the landscape. I want to walk along the erratic passage through crumbling rock with the softest of footsteps. Like the gorge, I feel cracked, altered, and exposed, opened wide for all to see.

Most of all, I want to be reminded of how Earth heals and life continues following disturbance. I want to surround myself in Earth's resilience.

There are six major types of faults, according to my new geology book. I bought the book because, according to the online description, it features "clear graphics and simple field-guide procedures to guide hikers through the great outdoors." I am optimistic that, along with Hailey, it will lead me to a fault.

The majority of faults in the BFZ are normal faults, formed when rocks stretch and break under immense pressure. The difference between a crack and a fault is that a fault is followed by movement and, in extreme cases, an earthquake.

As blocks of rock, or units, move independently, they push against one other, as if vying for space. Eventually, one unit of rock will drop and the other will rise. Displaced. I remember this feeling too, when I first moved to Texas. Everything seemed vaguely familiar, but different—the birds, the plants, the butterflies. Here in the gorge, subterranean forces moved rocks, causing them to shift and crack and form uneven layers, blurring the passage of time. But, unlike California's infamous San Andreas Fault, the Balcones Fault is dormant.

But what would an actual fault look like? How would a geologist recognize it, as she gazed out over the rocky, uneven terrain? I set out today to walk the gorge like a geologist reading a new, yet ancient, landscape.

Just beyond the dam at the beginning of the spillway, our group encounters tracks from a carnivorous dinosaur, *Acrocanthosaurus*. Her footprints were preserved in the muck of a muddy shoreline. Ryland places his foot in the depression and stretches his left leg to reach the next indentation, at least ten times bigger than his own shoe. He steps to the next one and the next, re-creating the stride of a dinosaur a third the size of *Tyranno-saurus rex.*

Farther down the gorge, a loose layer of white shells, the shape and size of an infant's fingernail, cover the ground. They crunch beneath my feet. The shells, Hailey points out, belong to single-celled *Foraminifera*, an ancient amoeba-like protist that formed a complex shell for protection. Ryland picks up an apple-sized rock and, with his fingers, digs out more *Foraminifera* from the crumbling edges, a perfect example of how the limestone formed long ago. I take his picture with the shells in one hand and the rock in the other, a reminder that every inch of the gorge reveals clues to the past.

The key to finding a fault, I learn from Hailey, is to notice change. Sometimes a change can be subtle, sometimes abrupt. Early in the hike, our group reaches an area that is rust-colored and cratered, so unusual it makes me feel as if I have stepped onto the surface of another planet. Ancient clams created this terrain as they poked holes in the surface to extend tubes for feeding and eliminating waste. Hailey tells us it is called bored hardground.

Moving downhill, the terrain changes again and the bored hardground disappears. Near the end of the hike Hailey suddenly exclaims, "Remember how I told you to keep the bored hardground in mind?" She points at the ground, and there, beneath our feet, the rough ground suddenly appears again. Hailey explains that this shift in terrain suggests a fault exists between the two areas of hardground. The missing middle section of hardground sank beneath the surface long ago.

On the other side of the gorge, I step over what looks like a terraced balcony, with narrow raised ridges, less than the width of my foot and nearly the length of my body. Made of slate-colored limestone, the ridges run in parallel directions. They resemble the backs of whales arching above the ocean's surface as they descend on a deep dive. Ryland jumps from ridge to ridge, one foot in front of the other, as if on a balance beam.

Kneeling down, Hailey points to a series of slickensides, which I would have overlooked. These shiny, smooth surfaces on the sides of the ridges were created when rocks slid past one another. Small parallel lines look like cat scratches. This is the site of many small faults where the ridges rose, and the spaces in between sank and later filled with silt.

I expected a fault to be dramatic, a deep, extensive hole in the ground, something visible, something impossible to overlook—a place where I might fall over the edge. But not all faults or wounds are easily identified, much like the tiniest cracks in life that branch and spread until, one day, everything shatters.

The trick, it seems, is to accept change, however small, to sit with it, and to see what the cracks reveal.

LOST LAYERS

Loved ones who passed away:

6 years ago, Aunt Diana
5 years ago, Uncle Doug
4 years ago, Roy, my husband's stepfather
3 years ago, Uncle Sonny
2 years ago, Marigan, my mother
2 years ago, Kyle, my cousin
1 year ago, Michael, my father
1 year ago, Uncle Jimmie

Two months ago, I helped pack my oldest son's belongings and drove him to college. Closing the door behind us, I let go of the small, blond boy crouched beneath his preschool chair, the long-legged boy perched in front of his computer, the curly-headed young man playing his trombone to a packed stadium. Although my mind knows differently, my heart experiences this as loss—a time passed, another layer finished and left behind.

Before long, my middle son will go, and then my youngest, Ryland, too, leaving behind holes in our family layers.

MISSING LAYERS

All caves are hollowed-out spaces, but that is where the similarity ends. Across the planet, caves are diverse. There are sea caves and caves with disappearing rivers. There are caves that flood seasonally and caves that remain dry. There are caves that boast intriguing titles like the deepest (the underground Everest) or the longest or the oldest. There are wild caves, where creatures go about their lives, and show caves, where people walk along lighted paths to learn about the subterranean world. There are active caves, where stalactites and stalagmites grow, and fossil caves that have remained unchanged for billions of years. There are caves carved from limestone, and caves formed from fallen granite boulders. There are caves that form when rainwater flows downward into the ground, and caves that form from groundwater rising from below. There are caves carved by the wind, and caves carved by hot gases, like sulfur. And I hope there are hidden caves, untouched by humans.

In Central Texas, there are more than three thousand caves, each with its own origin story, history, and unique structure. Caves are found throughout karst terrain, which covers more than 20 percent of the state. Cavers and cave scientists, or speleologists, believe that many more exist.

Caves in karst terrain form near faults, often as offshoots of major faults. Where there are cracks, water flows and mixes with limestone, producing an acid. The weak acid dissolves the rock, leaving behind holes that grow bigger and bigger over time.

When a hole leads to a cavern big enough for a human being to enter, it is called a cave. Although caves are voids, they hold many things—water, history, life, stories, secrets—like human beings.

WET LAYERS

Rocks of various shapes and sizes sit atop side-by-side picnic tables. "I promise I won't bore you with geology," our guide chuckles. A soft-spoken man, Jim is a Texas Master Naturalist (TMN) and, as I'm thrilled to learn, a retired geologist. "Yes, please do," I chime in as we gather round the picnic tables. Our group is made up of two families, an older couple, and me. Jim's wife, also a TMN, encourages us to hold the rocks, peer through the holes, and feel the chalky residue they leave behind.

Today I am visiting Honey Creek Cave State Natural Area, an offshoot of the Guadalupe River State Park, located in Spring Branch, Texas, thirty-five miles from my home. Jim explains that this isn't the best hike for learning about geology because so much is hidden beneath our feet, but, whenever possible, he sneaks in geology facts.

As we hike through dry savannas and juniper forests, I ask Jim about Honey Creek Cave, the real reason for my visit. I know the cave is on private property, but I am hoping for a glimpse, or at least the opportunity to walk over the top of the cave, imagining its meandering tunnels below. Jim informs me, "We won't get anywhere near it." Although I feel disappointed, I understand that some things must remain hidden, for protection.

Near the edges of the creek, we spot enormous boulders scattered among the tall grasses, as if something has collapsed, like ruins. "You are looking at part of the Trinity Aquifer," Jim shares with us. The boulders have been exposed by the carving of the river. Further down the creek, I later learn, the first entrance to the cave is located in a pile of boulders similar to this one. The other entrance is a man-made shaft marked at the surface by a metal plate similar to a manhole cover.

Because of the challenges of entering and navigating through Honey Creek Cave, it is only an option for expert cavers. An expert caver I am not, not even close, and so I do the next best thing, for now: I curl up with a steaming cup of jasmine tea and hit the play button on my computer screen.

The YouTube video expedition, known as the Honey Creek Cave Extravaganza, begins on a chilly winter morning. A group of highly experienced cavers and cave scientists huddle near the shaft that leads down into the watery depths of Honey Creek Cave. Led by speleologist Jean "The Creature" Krejca, a legend in the field, and James Brown, they ready for the mission of mapping the virgin regions of the cave.

Honey Creek Cave is a water pathway, a flowpath, through the Trinity Aquifer. Aquifers are areas of rock—fractures, holes, and caverns—where water collects, sometimes in vast quantities. In Central Texas and in karst regions all over the planet, aquifers provide drinking water. By mapping wet caves like this one, scientists gain a better understanding of how water flows through an aquifer—velocities, pathways, and destinations—a field of science known as geohydrology. These data then inform decisions about water conservation.

A tractor lowers the team members on a rope, three at a time, 140 feet down a narrow shaft into the cave. From there the team carries packs filled with diving equipment and other tools needed for their expedition. When the water gets deep, they tie the packs to their waists with rope. Using neon-yellow knotted rope attached to rock at points along the way to guide them through the murky waters and dark corridors, they take six hours to move three and a half miles.

Some passages are air-filled and team members wade through chin-level water, tilting their heads upward to breathe. Other passages, which dip below the water table into an area known as the phreatic zone, are completely submerged. The team makes their way, swimming and crawling through narrow spaces, surrounded by sharp rocks. Covered in thick, clay-like mud from head to toe, they stop to set up camp. The group finds ledges and depressions in the rock where they nestle in for the night, half-hidden, alongside the other creatures—salamanders and crickets and harvestmen—that call the cave home.

The next day, using ropes and a compass, Krejca and Brown reach their destination and map more than two thousand feet of new passage. They discover an unmapped sump, a submerged area that requires diving equipment and oxygen. When passages and waterways are mapped, cave scientists note the depth and location of the water, and also where water enters and exits the cave, through springs and seeps.

Using computer programs, like Walls or Compass, scientists map caves in 3D. They create overlapping layers that represent different cave features: geological layers, biological layers, and hydrological layers. Later other scientists can view the cave as a whole or examine the separate layers.

Much of Honey Creek Cave is still unmapped. No one knows where its passages may lead.

MYSTERIOUS LAYERS

Last fall, something unusual showed up in my annual bloodwork, something concerning. *How was I feeling*, my doctor wanted to know. *The usual*, I told her, what I'd come to expect, what I thought was typical for a woman my age: tired, a little achy, not myself.

Two years ago, I made a doctor's appointment because I felt unusually tired, like I was falling in slow motion down a hole with no end. I could barely keep my eyes open while driving or writing or doing daily tasks. Exhaustion wrapped itself around me like a straitjacket.

Fatigue is the most common complaint among middle-aged women. It is a symptom with endless possibilities, which makes diagnosis tricky. I also have Graves' disease, a thyroid condition that can fluctuate without warning, making me feel like a stranger in my own body. "Are you depressed?" my doctor probed. I stopped to think. No, I didn't feel depressed. The next week, I participated in a sleep study, but sleep apnea was ruled out. If I lost weight and exercised more, things should improve.

Now my blood test showed that I was severely anemic. There wasn't enough iron in my body to produce hemoglobin, a part of the red blood cell necessary for transporting oxygen. My red blood cells were misshapen, too small, due to the absence of hemoglobin. Because the majority of iron in the human body is recycled from old blood cells, low levels of iron indicate abnormal blood loss.

"We need a plan," my doctor explained over the phone. "We need to find the source of the bleed."

I was bleeding from somewhere deep inside the unexplored and unmapped areas of my own body. I thought the doctor would prescribe an iron supplement, and life would continue as usual. I was wrong.

The most common sources of internal bleeding are the stomach, bowel, or uterus. The cause is frequently cancer. Visits with specialists followed by tests, procedures, and scans lasted for five months. Glancing up from the computer screen, each specialist inquired about my family history, as if I had overlooked that section. I explained, again and again, that my health history was vague because, as an infant, I was adopted. As I tell my sons, there are a few mystery genes in the mix.

When a patient doesn't have access to their family history, some doctors get nervous. Like a road map, family history guides physicians to problems that a patient is prone to developing. In my case, the information needed to make sense of the situation was missing. I understood. I often felt incomplete, like a puzzle with scattered pieces somewhere just out of reach.

As I learned, for adoptees many tests, including mammograms and colonoscopies, should be done long before the recommended age, just in case. I panicked. Had I not been taking care of myself? Was this my fault?

After each test, each procedure, the results returned: normal. The doctors found nothing, nothing they could see or analyze or make sense of; sometimes science is like that, no matter how hard we try to sort things through, there is no answer.

Months later, watching an iron-infused fluid drip from a bag and into my veins, I finally let exhaustion flow through me instead of running in the other direction. I sat in a room, untouched books piled on my lap, with strangers who were receiving cancer treatments, alone because of COVID-19. There was a certain silence about the room despite the machines humming and nurses whispering, a certain emptiness as we all sat together. I closed my eyes. I thought of my father the year before, receiving his cancer treatments in a place just like this, alone. I knew I would be okay, but I cried for the strangers and their uncertain futures. It was all I could do.

The only conclusion that could be made was that my anemia was the result of heavy menstrual bleeding, a condition treated with hormones. But I continue to check in with the doctors, just in case. Without a family history, some things remain a mystery.

COLLAPSED LAYERS

I step backward, terrified to set foot onto the metal platform that extends out and over Devil's Sinkhole into nothingness. My husband reaches for the camera, and without hesitation, I pass it to him. Ryland follows, and from the platform's farthest edge, my husband leans over the railing, angling the camera downward to get a shot of the enormous sinkhole. Nearly fifty feet wide, the opening would fit two school buses across it; at more than 350 feet deep, the sinkhole is as deep as a football field is long. I can't watch.

Later, feet firmly on grass-covered ground, I stare at the camera screen in awe: a tunnel of darkness, like staring down the throat of a giant. At times my fear of heights holds me back, but then heightens my curiosity.

A hole, like a cave, is often seen as empty space, the abyss, devoid of life. It is a place where something existed that now is lost. But today, overhead, cave swallows swoop and dive, catching insects in their beaks, midair. Maidenhair ferns, like Rapunzel's long locks, tumble down the sides, softening the rough edges. Male bats roost inside the cave, a true man cave, that extends farther back from the giant hole. Life bursts from emptiness.

Although the sinkhole and connected cave, located in Rocksprings, Texas, are not open to the public, they are the site of many expeditions. Skilled vertical climbers rappel down into the shaft entrance in search of lost bat rooms, the source of rumors. Researchers study Mexican free-tailed bats, one of the largest populations in the world. Cave divers explore the lake rooms, two rooms submerged under water.

Caves are often discovered when the surrounding ground collapses or, more often, when water, over thousands of years, carves a channel downward toward a small opening. Over time, the newly formed basin grows bigger and bigger as soil slides down the angled sides, forming a sinkhole.

There is a theme that reveals itself again and again as I explore the Hill Country: there are lessons to be learned and new things to be found following a natural disturbance. I tuck this bit of knowledge away, sure that it will come in handy.

The earliest record of Devil's Sinkhole is from 1889. Like Devil's Sinkhole, many historical features in the Hill Country have names that suggest fear: Purgatory Road, Devil's Hollow, Devil's Backbone, Witches' Fingers, Devil's River, Phantom Cave. Throughout human history, the subterranean has been viewed as a portal to a dark underworld. For others, like me, caves and sinkholes elicit a fear of tight spaces, a fear of falling, and a fear of heights. In the Hill Country, there is also a history of filling holes and caves for various reasons, but I believe it all boils down to a fear of the unknown.

Weeks later, while kayaking around Spring Lake, I learn from a college student and guide that local Indigenous groups view the subterranean in a different way, as part of their origin story. The Coahuiltecan of San Marcos believe that their ancestors followed deer to the surface from the underworld. As marked by annual ceremonies, the subterranean is where life began.

Although fear once named this rocky landscape, I seek out stories of connection—intimate relationships between rock and water and living things. Connections grow between layers, like roots.

Scientists are also working to shed light in the darkness, so that people no longer fear the depths. They study geology, hydrology, and the living things that call groundwater, caves, cracks, and crevices home. They locate filled caves and sinkholes and excavate them, allowing water to flow freely and fill the aquifers. Since moving to the Hill Country and finding home in this rocky terrain, I feel compelled to deepen my relationship with the subterranean, to explore my connection to it and the need to protect it.

INTERTWINED LAYERS

In his book *The Hidden Life of Trees*, Peter Wohlleben shares research on how trees communicate. As it turns out, leaves, roots, and fungi work together to survive, relying more on cooperation than competition. Root networks use chemical communication among different species, signaling drought or disease. And, as I taught my biology students, leaves clinging to the highest branches rely on water and nutrients from roots far below; roots deep belowground rely on sugars made by leaves high above.

Scientists studying karst systems in Texas have discovered that roots grow into caves. Like fungal mycelium, the branch-like filaments that form extensive mats beneath the surface, oak roots and Ashe juniper roots extend into caves. The roots seek out water and nutrients trapped in cracks and crevices. The roots of different species twist and turn, squeezing through the earth together, so closely intertwined that the only thing that differentiates one species from another is its DNA.

Around a family fire pit on a Taco Tuesday, several women from Ryland's Montessori school discover we have all recently read *The Hidden Life of Trees*. We talk about tree communication and how it relates to school communities, as our children run through the juniper forest, hooting and hollering, leaving their tacos to grow cold. We talk about the toll the pandemic has taken on the teachers and the children and the parents, our well of resources depleted. We talk about feeling isolated from one another. We talk about the things we miss: holiday potlucks, school-wide picnics, music with Ms. Sarah on Friday mornings. We talk about the growing need to come together, to intertwine.

FRAGILE LAYERS

On a hilltop, loose gravel slips away beneath my feet, bouncing off broken ledges as it falls. The soil is so thin I am unsure it can be classified as soil, more like crushed rock. This fragile layer, as thin as aging skin, acts as a boundary between two worlds, the surface and the subterranean. Some people refer to this layer as karst skin.

Because of the steep incline, rainwater and wind easily wash away the soil. Wind is a frequent visitor. Trees, like Ashe juniper and live oak, are short and misshapen, often leaning to one side as if caught in a game of freeze tag with the wind. I know this place well. It is part of the land my family owns, where one day, we will build new layers.

Plants with shallow root systems dot the hillside. Clump grasses burst from cracks and crevices every now and then alongside the occasional prickly pear cactus or yucca plant, with its sword-like leaves. At first this land seems barren, scrubby, a place no one would want to buy, unsuitable for a home because of the steep drop-off into the canyon. But, after every visit and with patience and over time, the land gets to know us and reveals her secrets.

I stop to collect a withered coil of blue-green algae (cyanobacteria), something I had originally mistaken for desiccated scat. I place it in Ryland's hand and pour water over it. We watch as the mass plumpens. Similarly, after rain, the colony of single-celled cyanobacteria swells until it looks like a piece of dark brown rubber often called witches'-butter (*Nostoc commune*). It tastes like seaweed, I've been told. I find it scattered across the hillside.

Under my feet, the soil crunches. Moon-white cups, much smaller than my pinky nail, blanket the soil and rock fragments. Using iNaturalist, I identify the lichen as brick scale lichen (*Psora crenata*). So prolific, portions of the hillside look like they are covered in snow.

These organisms are part of the biocrust, a thin layer that brings life to dirt or dirt to life, creating soil. They are the first organisms to colonize bare ground and include lichens, mosses, microfungi, and bacteria. Their job is an important one: they fertilize and stabilize soil, and help retain moisture. Although they are studied extensively in deserts and extremely cold environments around the world, biocrusts are not well understood in karst regions.

CAVE LAYERS

Colin Strickland, a biologist with the Balcones Canyonlands Preserve in Austin, is the son of caving legends. He grew up in caves. His wife is a caver, well known for her ability to squeeze into tight spaces and move dirt from filled passageways at a high rate of speed. His young children are growing up in caves, too. At work, he surveys caves, paying close attention to the living things he finds dwelling there.

At the annual National Caves and Karst Management Symposium in San Marcos, Texas, cavers and cave scientists pack into a ballroom and squirm in generic chairs while waiting to see what Strickland has been up to in the past year. Over the summer, Strickland presented to our Master Naturalist group, and so I am excited to hear him again. I know this will be anything but the usual presentation describing findings from a scientific journal. While we wait, see-through salamanders, pseudoscorpions with long, narrow pincers, and other ghostly white creatures surround us, their larger-than-life photographs staring back from tripods placed around the room.

As Strickland steps up to the podium, his quiet demeanor is evident. I begin to wonder if the ponytailed young man is uncomfortable with the bright lighting. Soon the lights dim and he takes us on a virtual journey from the surface entrance of a cave down into the depths, with videos and pictures and music.

The first video captures a cave entrance at night. Water-loving ferns and mosses flourish and just beyond, the branches of holly and persimmon trees provide food for foraging creatures. Every night hungry predators, like porcupines, lurk at cave entrances, waiting for what emerges. Their favorite snack appears to be the cave crickets that flood out of the cave in vast numbers.

Troglophiles are organisms that don't rely on caves but use them as temporary shelters. Toads, western slimy salamanders, crickets, land slugs, and snails fall into this category. They escape the summer heat and winter cold inside caves, leaving only to forage.

Deeper in the cave, trogloxenes are cave guests who visit during a part of their life cycle. Some bat species use caves to hibernate or raise their young. Harvestmen overwinter in basketball-sized clusters. Raccoons, gray foxes, ringtails, and bobcats may also use caves from time to time, often to raise their young.

In the darkest reaches of the cave, troglobites, who can't survive on the surface, spend their entire life cycle in caves. Certain species of pseudoscorpions, millipedes, beetles, spiders, and silverfish are some of the creatures that fall into this category. A range of adaptations—small size, slow metabolism, long legs, and limited egg production—allows them to survive in the most extreme areas of caves. Troglobites, like snails, have antennae that can sense chemicals in the environment and they use this information to find food and to navigate in darkness.

Strickland cues up one of his favorite videos from his YouTube channel, *BioSubterranea*. In the darkness, a pseudoscorpion (*Tartarocreagris infernalis*), smaller than a dime, waves its long pincers, appendages that resemble lobster claws. It lacks a venomous tail like true scorpions and it is blind, like many other cave-dwelling invertebrates. A tactile creature, the pseudoscorpion relies on sensory hairs found on its legs and pincers to catch prey. The action happens in slow motion. First the pseudoscorpion's pincer hairs brush against something, indicating that dinner is nearby. It is an unlucky eyeless spider. It escapes, just in time.

The pseudoscorpion waits. Eerie synthesizer music elevates the tension of the unfolding drama. The two creatures are within centimeters of one another. Then the spider stumbles right into its predator. With the spider in the tight grasp of one pincer, the pseudoscorpion punctures the spider's abdomen and injects venom from a gland in the other pincer. The drama comes to an end.

A young woman, a caver, leans over to whisper that Strickland tells audiences what kind of camera he uses, the exact make and model. She bought one. She laughs as she confesses, "None of my pictures look anything like that."

In the dark, wet karst layers of the subterranean, another community of animals known as stygobites go about their mysterious lives, unseen. Named after the River Styx, these creatures include populations of soft-bodied animals like snails and worms that are neighbors with salamanders and a few fish species. There are also beetles, but few other insects. And there are many crustaceans, isopods and amphipods, invertebrates with hard exoskeletons that are related to shrimp. Ben Hutchins of Texas State University studies these creatures, presenting his work alongside Strickland.

The creatures live in tight, submerged spaces between cracks, in cave streams, and in holes and caverns where groundwater flows. They have adapted to this strange life in a variety of ways. Some are skinny and long-legged, others stocky, but they all tend to be eyeless and have lost their pigmentation, giving them a ghostlike appearance.

Because caves are dark, plants cannot photosynthesize in them and thus are not part of the cave ecosystem. So how do all of these animals find food? Nutrients can be washed into caves in the form of leaves or sticks, and sometimes animals wander into caves and die. Dissolved matter in rainwater also filters down through the rocks. Bacteria, like microscopic magicians, build their bodies using energy from inorganic materials like sulfur and nitrogen. Their bodies form colonies with strange appearances: stringy mats or slimy sheets. Bacterial colonies become food for hungry invertebrates.

But finding resources is always a challenge for isolated critters. In dry caves where bats roost, the food web begins in bat guano. Microbes and beetles rely on guano as a source of energy and the web builds from there, branching out to include harvestmen and spiders. In caves where bats are absent, cave crickets, insects that travel in and out of the cave, leave their waste behind. The waste layer becomes the basis of the food web in the same way as bat guano.

Scientists like Strickland and Hutchins work to develop new methods for studying karst creatures. Not long ago, little was known about subterranean ecosystems, but these researchers' work is opening new windows into that world. Hutchins likens his work to documenting the unknown, like an explorer. Collecting, identifying, and classifying newly discovered creatures is like creating a living map of caves.

GROWING LAYERS

When I was pregnant, I tried to imagine all the layers growing and rearranging themselves inside my body: atoms, molecules, cells, tissues, organ, organ systems. Layers forming below the surface, in a place as dark and remote as a cave.

As my children grew, I lived through the everyday dramas of the many developmental stages: the pain of getting a foot stuck between the slats in the playground bridge, the fear of entering a classroom filled with strangers, the embarrassment of answering a question wrong or wearing geeky shoes, the frustration of not making the team, or the anguish of losing a girlfriend—all the things that will seem small someday, tiny cracks, that in the moment, felt like faults forming in my heart.

I remember the shock of a new feeling—the way every time my children ventured into the world, it was as if I were exposing the most raw and vulnerable parts of myself; as if somewhere, deep inside, mother and child were still connected by a watery pathway of cells and blood and tears.

BEDROCK LAYERS

In my yard, I create habitat by planting for wildlife—insects, birds, and small mammals. I started more than ten years ago after attending a workshop at the Houston Arboretum. The main takeaway was to plant in layers, so that living things, in all their different shapes and sizes and with their diverse lifestyles, could find suitable food and shelter. I wrote this diagram in my notebook:

groundcover → understory (herbs, shrubs, vines) → canopy (taller trees)

Today I am hiking at the Westcave Outdoor Discovery Center in Round Mountain, Texas, forty-five miles from my home. I wish Ryland were here, but he is busy with his own investigation at school, drawing and naming the bones of the human body. I join a family from Massachusetts, a young couple, and a young photographer blogging about beautiful spots close to her home. As we descend a steep and winding rock staircase into the valley, our guide, a curious, intelligent, rock-climbing mother, asks us to observe the layers as we go.

It is as if the diagram from my old notebook has come to life. Near the river, mosses, ferns, and a variety of tiny wildflowers fill in the areas close to the ground. Turk's cap, with its tubular, fire-red flowers, and dwarf palmettos, small palm-like plants, form the understory, the middle ground. Bald cypress trees, hundreds of years old, tower above us, branches intertwining to form the canopy. And right in the middle of it all, a creek gurgles and gulps. A result of the wet environment, the tangled, jungle-like place before me sits in stark contrast to the dry savanna where we began our hike.

At the head of a lush canyon, our group stops at a spectacular site where spring water gushes from rock, mixes with creek water from above, and creates a waterfall. I learn about an accidental experiment that reveals secrets about the aboveground layers. In the past, visitors would sit on a group of boulders while listening to a guide talk about the cave nearby. The rocks were bare. Then a rope boundary was constructed. Over the next several years, life took hold. Today the rocks are covered in layers of ferns and mosses.

The Bryophytes of Texas, an iNaturalist project, focuses on the special group of plants called bryophytes, including liverworts and mosses, that grow on top of other things. This branch of ecology is known as substrate ecology. Because these primitive plants lack true roots to push down into the soil, they grow on top of trees and soil, rock and leaf litter. Some bryophytes, the epiphylls, grow on leaves; epiphytes grow on tree trunks or stems; and others, called epiliths, grow on rock.

If I stop at any point along the way and peel back the layers, I will find rock. Rock is at the heart of everything in the Hill Country. As a mother, I dream of being like that rock, a place from where my family grows, building their own layers as they go.

HUMAN LAYERS

Like an archaeologist carries tools, I carry questions. Should I have moved closer to family? Could I have helped more? Was I a good daughter? Am I ready to step into the role of family leader, the wise, older woman like my mother? Will I be strong enough to hold us all together as our family structure shifts, as the landscape beyond our door shifts?

As I dig, I collect memories and stories, like fossils and bones, piecing together fragments, one by one. I unearth objects—rocks, shells, an enormous pottery bowl—from boxes filled with the stuff of lives lived. I place these objects on shelves, just so, like a museum. Each object evokes images. I see them, my mother and father, my aunts and uncles, my cousin; they drift through my days, full of color and laughter and life. I remain deep in the layers of the past where I feel their presence, so they won't be left behind.

As I crawl through the crumbling spaces, I try to stabilize what remains. I try to draw elaborate maps of the past and of the future in my mind. As if I am constructing a game of Jenga, I try to arrange pieces into layers, neatly stacked, one on top of the other, acutely aware of the cracks and faults and empty spaces. I am unsure where this work will lead or when it will end. Even for geologists, stratigraphy is rarely simple.

I step back every now and then, to observe my work and to listen for signs of life in the layers. Worries rise to the surface and spill over, filling in cracks and forming new ones. I worry about the future, about my sons and about this vulnerable place of limestone and water. Will the growing population learn about the need for stewardship? Will they learn about the connection between the surface and the subsurface? Will they protect what cannot be seen, the unexplored and unexplained places?

At a birthday party for Ryland's friend the day before Halloween, friends ask what else we have planned for the holiday. Later that night, we are headed to a spooktacular performance with scary stories and music in a cave one hundred feet below the surface. My husband rolls his eyes and comments, "She rarely spends time aboveground now." Although I laugh at the familiar jab, the possibility of that statement hangs in the air. Sometimes I worry that I spend too much time wandering belowground, searching through the past. I wonder if I have forgotten to build upward.

THE RECHARGE
ZONE

Nothing went as planned that October morning. It was supposed to be my first visit to a wild Texas cave. Fighting wind gusts, cavers loaded ropes, helmets, and headlamps into the van. Swiftly moving clouds gathered overhead, making the sky slate gray, as if morning had turned to night. The temperature plummeted thirty degrees overnight, transporting me from a balmy evening the night before to the first chilly morning of the season. I stood to the side watching, wearing lightweight hiking pants, a short-sleeved shirt, and a flimsy jacket, wondering what I had gotten myself into.

The field trip, titled "Finding Caves and Sinkholes," was part of the National Cave and Karst Management Symposium. I had been searching for caves near my home, and although I was excited to glean new tips from the outing that might point me in the right direction, worries flooded my mind: I was afraid of heights; I was afraid of tight spaces; heck, in that moment, I wondered if I might be afraid of the dark too. But there I stood, nearby professional cavers, hydrologists, geologists, and cave scientists, a middle-aged, fairly out-of-shape woman totally unprepared for the day ahead. I gritted my teeth and resisted the urge to run.

Heavy raindrops pounded the van's windshield on the way to our first destination. From behind the steering wheel, our trip leader, Nico Hauwert, a local hydrogeologist, announced a change of plans. Due to the recent death of Hauwert's friend and the landowner, we no longer had access to the sinkholes. Instead we would visit a sinkhole on the edge of a ranch remnant that had become surrounded by sprawling housing developments. As we traipsed through a field, the wind picked up again. Thunder cracked. We walked in silence beneath hoods and umbrellas with rainwater rushing in streams over our boots. Before long, the rivulets surrounded us.

Still, we plodded onward to the edge of a sinkhole, where seven of us crowded around a steel railing and stared down into the rocky abyss. Rain-soaked, numb, and distracted by my discomfort, I committed little of the sinkhole to memory, just that it was smaller than I expected, more like a bathtub. Easily overlooked. All I could do was stand in awe of the water, how it possessed the power to carve its own path through the fragmented terrain.

Back in the van, Hauwert changed plans again. Conditions had become too treacherous for us to descend into the cave that had been selected, but he wanted to show us something else. It was the perfect day, he promised. I was doubtful. Over the frantic thud of the windshield wipers, he spoke of water flow pathways. Water travels fast through karst terrain, faster than was previously suspected. Hauwert knew this firsthand because he had performed water tracing tests—placing dye in the water and seeing when and where it turned up downstream. On stormy days water *rushed* up, down, over, and under the rocky terrain.

At the next stop, we hiked to the edge of Onion Creek. By that time the rain was falling in sheets. We took turns standing next to Hauwert on a crumbling ledge. When it was my turn, I trod through tangled bushes and thorny vines, pushing aside persimmon branches and finding tenuous footing on toppled grasses. I peered cautiously over the bank to the creek more than six feet below, the drop steep enough to send chills through my body.

All summer the creek bed had been dry, but in the middle of the storm, the thunderous gush of water nearly drowned out Hauwert's voice. He pointed along the creek's edges to whirlpools that formed. They sounded like someone chugging water. "Swallets!" he yelled more than once before the unfamiliar word reached my ears. Swallets—about sixteen of them—lined the sides of Onion Creek, he explained, each one no bigger than a manhole cover. The opposite of springs, swallets are holes where water enters and travels deep down into the labyrinthine channels of the subterranean. The water made choppy, gurgling noises, as if the creek was choking, struggling to come back to life.

Vulnerable areas of karst terrain with aquifers just below the surface, like the Onion Creek watershed, are known as recharge zones. Holes, like swallets, and other faults and fractures are crucial features, Hauwert explained. Because water moves rapidly over the surface of this kind of landscape, there need to be catchment areas, places where the water slows, filters downward, and refills or recharges the aquifer. I had recognized that need in myself lately: the need to slow down, pause, let my body and mind recharge.

For a long time, I stood in silence, feet anchored in the recharge zone, witnessing the karst terrain transform. The storms, inevitable and necessary, had set everything in motion. I hadn't been prepared to experience it, but I couldn't turn away. I let it rush over me—the chaos of a harsh, wild, and unexpected storm. It was all I could do.

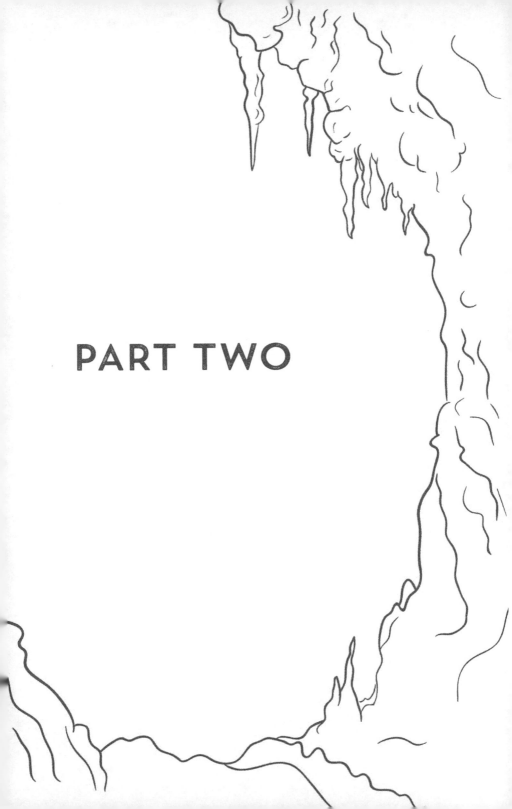

PART TWO

RETURNING HOME

On a late September evening, an ordinary Tuesday—or so it seems at first—I gather with strangers, eyes fixed on the mouth of a cave, as if we are waiting for the cave to speak, to share its secrets.

The cave entrance, shaped like an upside-down jack-o'-lantern grin, beckons like a passage to an ancient world. It lies at the bottom of a bowl, a sinkhole wide enough and deep enough to hold my home. Sporadic clumps of grasses and clusters of cacti peek out from between cracked rock. They cover the top of the cave and carpet the sinkhole floor and walls. But the entrance seems strangely empty, like a deep, dark void.

Twilight passes as I wait, seated on the edge of a limestone ledge. The land surrounding the cave is still. Not even a breeze stirs the dried grasses or shakes the leaves of the scraggly persimmon trees.

A peculiar odor hangs in the air. It seeps into the surroundings, clinging like Spanish moss on bent branches. Even the rocks soak up the smell. The scent, an odd mixture of moldy hay, decay, and ammonia, signals that bats are near.

A maternal colony of Mexican free-tailed bats (*Tadarida brasiliensis*), one of the largest in the world, makes its home here in Bracken Cave. As many as 20 million individuals roost on the cave ceilings at a time. For thousands of years bat mothers have returned in the spring to give birth and raise their young. The cave offers shelter: a nursery, a sanctuary, a home.

The setting sun weaves patterns in the sky. Wispy clouds, like cotton strands unfurling from spools, form colorful patterns that fade from blazing orange to grapefruit pink to lavender—the only sign that time has passed. I listen for motorcycles roaring or dogs barking or children playing, but I don't hear the familiar evening sounds that I do at my own house, just twenty miles away. San Antonio is thirty miles in the opposite direction. Given my location, to feel removed from the rest of the world, as if I am in the middle of nowhere, is remarkable. But I do not feel alone; I feel connected, part of something I cannot yet name.

It has been more than two years since I lost my mother, but it seems much longer. Years before a stroke took her life, dementia crept in, altering the pathways of her mind, until one day even my name became something difficult to find. Ever so slowly, my mother slipped away, like a hummingbird caught in a storm, wild winds carrying her farther and farther from home.

As I watched illness enshroud her, I wondered how I would navigate the world without her. In the years since, I have learned to find my way. I see now that my mother gave me wings to fly, even in her absence. Yet something akin to loss still looms: a longing to return home, to be mothered.

Over the summer I meet my friend Rachel at the San Antonio Botanical Garden for a picnic. As our boys scour the hedgerows for imaginary monsters, I ask about her plans to return home to Vancouver. I know it has been on her mind. She and her son haven't seen her parents in more than a year because of the pandemic. Her baby daughter hasn't met her grandparents.

Rachel shifts, searches for a comfortable position on the picnic blanket, and then looks away. She stands instead, baby balancing on her hip, unsettled. A few nights earlier her daughter's passport arrived in the mail, she explains. They were ready to book a flight, but when she called her parents to share the good news they told her to put her visit on hold. Her mother announced, "We are selling the house."

After hanging up the phone, Rachel sobbed for hours. She seems embarrassed to admit this detail, repeating several times that it is just a house. Her husband has been out of town on business for months, and Rachel dreams of home: kayaking on the lake, hiking the forested mountain, reading, and writing while her parents spend time with their newest granddaughter.

I imagine Rachel hopes her mother will swoop in, take care of meals and bath time, tuck the children into bed and read them the same stories they read to her. Then, sinking into the cushions of a favorite couch, Rachel's mother will sit beside her in the quiet of the night, untangling the twisted threads of the past year.

Her mother will do this for Rachel because, like me, she will recognize the toll of motherhood, the exhaustion that grows alongside the joy. Rachel has pushed through a difficult year, waiting to be mothered.

I tell Rachel the story of how my father sold our family home soon after my mother died. The scene seared in my mind: My father sits in a chair where the kitchen table used to be, one hand on his cane, the other clinging to a tissue box in his lap. I stack dusty family albums and old records in boxes. I sweep floors. On a step stool, I remove wooden whales and stained-glass birds that hang over the bay window. I pack it all away, until all that remains is an empty space.

Some days I close my eyes and visit my childhood home. In my mind it isn't empty; it is just the way my mother left it. I know every room and doorway. I know the places where the flooring turns from carpet, to tile, to hardwood, and I know how it feels beneath my bare feet. I know the chest where my mother keeps hats and gloves and scarves, the closet crammed with extra sheets and blankets for guests, and the basement shelf where a red striped box holds ornaments awaiting Christmas.

In my mind, I sit at the counter on a barstool while my mother preps ingredients for spaghetti sauce. The staccato beat of a knife tapping a cutting board and the smell of sautéed onion fill the air. I tell her about what I am writing and how the kids are doing. I tell her about the next adventure my husband and I are planning. I talk for hours without worrying that I am boring, or self-centered, or petty. My mother always listens. I am always welcome.

I often return to my conversation with Rachel. Since then, she has delayed her trip two more times, once due to COVID travel restrictions following another surge and the next time waiting for her parents to get settled in their new place, a city condo far from the wild places of childhood. Six months later Rachel still hasn't made the journey home.

In 1992 Bat Conservation International purchased five acres of land that included Bracken Cave. Today, after many additional purchases, the organization protects nearly 1,500 acres in an effort to create a buffer between encroaching development and the cave. The organization, with the help of volunteers and scientists, has restored the land with native vegetation, making home for wildlife in nooks and crannies across the preserve. When it rains, water flows across the undeveloped land, free of pavement, winding its way belowground, through the rocky layers of the aquifer.

Master Naturalists play an important role at Bracken Cave Preserve. When I first moved to Houston more than twenty years ago, I signed up to become a Texas Master Naturalist because I felt disoriented. Birds and bugs and trees looked familiar but upon closer inspection were different from their East Coast relatives, the ones I had known since childhood. In my new yard, I wanted to address everyone by name. The Master Naturalist program helped me do that.

The program's mission is to educate a corps of volunteers who will return to their communities and share information about the natural world. They also assist scientists in gathering data, an activity known as citizen science. The program involves classroom training and field experiences. Almost every state has a Master Naturalist program nurturing thousands of new natural stewards every year.

On my first trip to Bracken Cave, I planned to attend as a Master Naturalist. The preserve needed help with a Bioblitz event, a survey of the plants and animals that call the preserve home. On the drive, early morning fog rolled in and rain pounded the road. There were no signs to lead me to the cave. Bat Conservation International doesn't want to draw attention to the special place. I couldn't find the driveway. After nearly thirty minutes of searching I returned home.

Tonight a tiny, temporary sign, low to the ground and stuck in the dirt at an angle, guides me down the long, curving driveway to the cave. A fake skeleton in a dilapidated jeep waves from the roadside. I pass several data collection stations, including a weather station. After parking, I am greeted by two Master Naturalists who introduce me to the story of bat mothers.

Each bat mother gives birth to one pup a year. Born blind, the baby weighs as much as a dime. Adults weigh as much as two quarters and are the size of my hands placed side by side. Bat mothers nurse their pups on and off throughout the day and return to the cave twice during the night to nurse. When they emerge, mothers feed on egg-laden moths, high in fat content, to maintain their energy reserves. Upon their return, a mother must find her pup in a dark, densely packed dome filled with thousands of other babies. Mothers do this by sound and smell, a testament to the bond of mother and child.

Just as the sun sinks below the horizon, a handful of people stream into the Bracken Cave viewing area, a group of rustic wooden benches arranged like an outdoor theater. Chatter fades. An older man unpacks his camera and tripod. Three young brothers, on hands and knees, encircle the base of a live oak tree, hunting lizards. A young girl spots a coral snake; the telltale pattern of maroon, mustard yellow, and black catches her eye. Her mother waves her arms to alert the rest of the group. Mother and daughter point and sound the alarm as best they can with hushed voices.

Soon rustling grasses near the cave entrance alert me to more movement. A raccoon waddles over the craggy terrain. A skunk appears from a thicket of Ashe juniper and meanders downhill toward the opening. Overhead, a great horned owl joins hawks and other raptors that float above the sinkhole, circling. A Master Naturalist, who is also circling and answering questions, shares with me that she has witnessed a rat snake slither across the top of the cave and drape itself down over the lip of the cave mouth, jaws at the ready. It is as if from somewhere, someone has whispered, "It's time."

I scoot to the edge of the rocky ledge and grab my new binoculars, a birthday gift from my husband. He is at home reading dragon stories to my youngest son, Ryland, and watching over our puppy. Before I leave, Ryland reminds me that dragons live in caves too, as if to say, *Be on the lookout, Mom.*

From the doorway, I glance back at Ryland sitting on his bed, dressed in his Pokémon pajamas with an oversized book, *Dragonology*, sprawled across his lap. I resist the urge to remind him that dragons aren't real. He is at that magical age where anything seems possible. Sometimes when I am with him I feel that way too.

Tonight I choose to be alone at Bracken Cave. I want to know this special place, a process that requires deep listening and the engagement of all my senses. And after a week of juggling schedules, including a parade, a high school football game, a county fair, and a birthday party, I am seeking silence and solitude—that elusive yet necessary part of motherhood.

* * *

"The only time I got stuck in a cave was the time I shoved my head through a small hole looking for bats." The white-haired man speaking leans against the wall of the conference room. He bites into a granola bar, dusting crumbs from his mustache. It seems as though everyone in the room turns to listen. The gentleman goes on to explain that getting his head through the tight space was no problem because, moving forward, his ears stayed flat against his head, but when he began backing out, the cave wall pulled his ears outward, preventing a safe exit.

Soon the lights dim. The elderly gentleman makes his way to the podium, and after I check to make sure his ears are intact, I am left wondering how he got out of his predicament. It is day two of the National Caves and Karst Management Symposium in San Marcos. I settle in to listen to a presentation titled "Cave Management for Bats."

The gentleman introduces himself as Merlin Tuttle. I look up from my notebook. I check the symposium schedule twice; this is not the presenter listed.

Tuttle is a legend, an ecologist, educator, and photographer who specializes in bat behavior and conservation. I remember that he was born the same year as my mother. He founded and for many years led Bat Conservation International, the same organization that oversees Bracken Cave. I have been reading his journal articles, following his blog, and learning about his work, a lengthy list of accomplishments spanning a lifetime. I can't believe my luck.

Tuttle begins by stating that, for all bat species, critical habitat is in jeopardy. For cave-dwelling bats, this means the number of suitable caves is in decline. The world is changing for this ancient species, and the reasons are varied. Landowners fill in caves to increase their property value for development. Ranchers dump trash in caves and sinkholes. Caves are sealed in an effort to kill bats, a result of fear. Caves may also be taken over by humans for tourism. When sites are lost, bats relocate. They end up traveling farther, decreasing their survival reserves.

Today bats are often found roosting in places Tuttle describes as "roosts of last resort," like bridges or attics or other human-made structures. Tuttle's protégé, Jim "Crash" Kennedy, joins the presentation to discuss the design and implementation of specialized bat gates, which protect bats from predation and disturbance. He explains that, for bats, there is a difference between surviving and prospering.

Is it a sudden breeze? A slight change in temperature or humidity? Is it the fading light or the shadows dancing on the cave walls? No one is quite sure what triggers the event, not even bat scientists, but in the instant I turn my head away from the cave, it happens, like an enormous exhale.

At first a sound like running water fills the space around me. I realize it is the rhythmic pattern of beating wings, a wild tempo. Near the cave entrance, thousands of bats emerge and swirl in a vortex, moving upward and counter-clockwise until they gain enough momentum to head east toward moth-filled fields. Each wing is made of a handlike skeleton with more than two dozen joints covered in a flexible membrane. Because of their wing structure, bats are skilled fliers, more adaptable and maneuverable than insects or birds. The serpentine shape of the bat vortex reminds me of Ryland's dragons, as if I am witnessing a dragon spring to life.

Despite the precision, the timing, and the physics of this ancient ritual, for some bats, the journey is short. It is a dangerous time; collisions are inevitable, especially when babies are learning to fly, as they are at this time of year. As the skunk and raccoon know, some bats will fall from the sky.

Once aloft, the bats maneuver erratically, darting and dodging, avoiding owls and other aerial predators that move in swiftly. Soon they form a steady stream and fly away at speeds of up to a hundred miles an hour. Tuttle refers to these bats affectionately as little jets. I watch as they climb, sometimes as high as ten thousand feet, until they are small specks in the distance.

I barely move from my perch, spellbound. The emergence can last as long as three hours. By early morning, the bats will return home to Bracken Cave.

When it comes to choosing a home, bats are nitpicky; their survival depends on it. Tuttle has learned that the cave's structure and location are critical. If their home is disturbed, bat mothers and fathers will search and search until they find a suitable dwelling.

The cave needs to be near food and water. It needs to be secure from predators. It must be able to maintain a stable temperature and have good airflow, which often requires multiple entrances. The entrances must be an appropriate size to allow for safe and efficient exit and reentry, something that varies by species. Some species prefer vegetation close to the entrance, like camouflage, while other species will not use a cave with overgrown vegetation because it interferes with their flight path. Hibernating bats need a dome-shaped, heat-trapping ceiling to roost. Baby bats require a humid environment for development. The roosting dome must be a certain distance from the cave entrance, depending on species. Bats need homes where they will not be disturbed, especially during hibernation. Disturbances cause them to waste resources needed to survive.

Tuttle has become so familiar with these needs that he can examine a cave map and predict where he will find bat colonies, or at least, where he should find them.

Tuttle has traveled the world to identify caves of historical importance, caves where bats once lived but are no longer found. Bats leave behind clues on cave ceilings. Carbon dioxide from bat breath, urine, and body oils etch the rock, forming dark stains where bats roost. Population size can be estimated by stain size.

Tuttle then decides what can be done in terms of cave recovery and restoration to encourage bats to return home.

The first step in cave recovery is education, something Tuttle is passionate about. He describes it as a matter of dispelling fears and convincing communities of the benefits of protecting bats. Bats provide ecological services like pest control for agricultural crops, seed dispersal, and pollination, and where bats dwell, tourism thrives, creating financial stability in remote communities. Tuttle shares pictures of places where he has worked his magic: Monfort Bat Cave, the Philippines; Cueva de la Boca, Mexico; Fern Cave, Alabama; Sneads Cave, Florida; and Porcupine Cave in Texas. As he travels the globe, bat populations grow in his wake.

Cave restoration is the process of making a cave a suitable home again. It may include removing overgrown vegetation from entrances, digging out buried entrances, or installing special bat gates to keep out predators and vandals. Spacious caverns with large openings draw humans, just like bats. Tuttle works with show cave owners, especially caves used for hibernation known as hibernacula. He has convinced owners to stop tours during the winter, to share space with hibernating bats. His message rings clear: cave recovery, restoration, and conservation require less work than people imagine.

Every year bats return to another Hill Country cave near my house. Unlike Bracken Cave, it is not composed of limestone but constructed of rebar, metal mesh, and gunite cement, a sticky, textured substance used to coat pools. From a dusty dirt road, a safe distance from the sleeping bats, I stare at the cave. Shaped like an igloo and tucked into the hillside, it resembles the entrance to a Disney ride, something strangely out of place in the middle of the tall grasses.

The artificial cave and summer bat home sits on a ranch named Selah, a Hebrew word meaning "stop, pause, and reflect." J.

David Bamberger, the original owner of the Church's Chicken franchise, bought the rundown, overgrazed ranch more than fifty years ago. Covered in aggressive plants and poor soil, the ranch needed help. Bamberger, with the assistance of scientists, friends, and volunteers, began restoring the land.

Today I am taking part in an opportunity, one of many, offered by staff and educators at the ranch: the Land Stewardship Workshop. Bamberger, nearly ninety years old, joins us to plant a sapling, a workshop tradition. Down to earth and overflowing with passion, he chats with us, telling stories of the trials and errors and years of hard work. His message of the day is one of hope, that with change the land heals. Looking out across acres of green, craggy hills, native grasses, creeks, and fall wildflowers, I can see how Bamberger's stories have transformed into reality.

In 1998 Bamberger visited Bracken Cave to view the bat emergence for the first time. He was awestruck. Private landowners still cared for the cave at the time. Inspired by his visit, he became a Bracken Cave committee chairman and a Bat Conservation International trustee, facilitating the purchase of the cave. He organized the construction of trails and the placement of interpretive signage and logs from which to view the bat journey. In limited numbers and with careful planning, guests were introduced to the bats. And then he did something else, something unexpected: he decided to transform his home, Selah, into a home for bats.

Because Bamberger never found limestone caves on Selah's five thousand acres, he set out to create a cave from scratch. In 2003 he assembled a team of experts, including an engineer and Merlin Tuttle, the bat conservation expert. The team searched for a suitable site, choosing a ravine where a cave could be cut into the hillside. The location would provide a clear flight path, access to water and insects, and an orientation conducive to capturing warm air.

The structure, shaped like a three-thousand-square-foot nautilus shell with three progressively larger, overlapping domes, provided eight thousand square feet of roosting surface. The final stage involved insulating the cave, burying it with soil, and planting native grasses over the top. Temperatures dropped twenty degrees within the cave, creating the ideal temperatures for nurturing bat babies.

From Tuttle, the team learned that the conditions inside the cave were just as critical as the structure. The surface needed to be textured but not too sharp for the bats to grasp with their claws. Eye hooks hung from the ceilings and crevices lined the walls. The team installed ventilation shafts to facilitate airflow and maintain stable temperatures. A large drainage pipe laid along the downward slope of the cave kept the cavern floor dry. The final touches included solar panels and a gate to keep out cattle. When the project was finally completed after seven months of design and construction, Bamberger christened the cave the chiroptorium, a combination of the word *chiroptera*, which means wing-handed, and the word *auditorium*.

For years the bats rejected the cave and it sat empty. The project became known as Bamberger's folly. With all of the specific requirements, a suitable human-made cave seemed like an impossibility, but Bamberger still believed in his cave. He and his team persisted, making adjustments here and there. And then they waited.

During that time, others attempted to construct artificial bat caves. The Nature Conservancy built a hibernaculum in Tennessee for gray bats that were dying at alarming rates. Bats were infected with white-nose syndrome, a disease that affects the muzzle and wings during hibernation. Bat specialists wondered if they could create a bat space that could be disinfected every spring in order to kill the fungus that causes the condition.

To test the idea, engineers designed and constructed an experimental cave next to an existing hibernaculum. The $300,000 project consisted of twenty-eight precast concrete sections like the ones used to construct culverts fitted together to form a long tunnel. A rainwater collection pipe maintained humidity levels within the cave and provided drinking water for bats. Loosely hanging fan belts and netting served as ideal roosting surfaces. Two entrances and several air chimneys helped with airflow and temperature regulation. Despite the careful attention to detail, including speakers that blasted ultrasonic bat calls, the bats rejected the cave.

Five years later, after a viewing window was covered on Bamberger's $50,000 chiroptorium, thousands of Mexican free-tailed bats found Selah, moved into the cave, gave birth, and raised their babies. The maternal colony has grown to include as many as 500,000 individuals, a fact that still feels like something of a miracle to me.

Having experienced the wonder of Bamberger's chiroptorium, I contact Crash Kennedy. I am still curious about the possibility of human-made bat caves. Kennedy is a pioneer and leader in the field of cave restoration, especially the installation of bat gates. When I ask about artificial caves, he describes another failed attempt in South Texas, one that he worked on. My guess is that cost along with the challenge of mimicking the structure and the specific conditions of a natural cave would limit experimentation. Kennedy confirms this and points out that, for success, the cave must be constructed on an enormous scale. "It's much easier to take better care of our existing caves than try to re-create nature from scratch," he says.

"People rarely conserve what they fear," Tuttle reminds us as his presentation comes to an end. In all his years spent in the presence of bats, he knows of only one person who contracted rabies, and that was a result of the vaccine. The incidence of disease transmission from bats to humans is dangerously exaggerated in the media, he believes. He never once had a bat entangle itself in his hair or try to suck his blood, but he has witnessed relentless fear-filled efforts to eradicate bats from homes all over the world.

My mind returns to the kitchen table at our summer cabin in Maine, a place that conjures stories of friends and relatives, bringing them back to life if only for a moment. One of our all-time favorite stories centers around my mother and a bat. In her absence, we clink wine glasses and retell the story, laughing and wiping tears from our cheeks.

One summer my mother had been staying at the cabin alone for a few days, waiting for the rest of us to arrive. While she was watching the news, she heard a noise and looked up. A lone bat fluttered near the top of the A-frame ceiling. She jumped up and opened all the doors and windows, but the bat stayed. She called her friends, who told her to go to bed and close the bedroom door. They would be over first thing in the morning.

It wasn't long before my mother awoke. She heard the bat fly-ing around the room. Unable to locate it in the darkness and too tired to do anything else, she opened the door and went back to sleep. In the morning her two friends arrived early with molasses donuts and steaming coffee and, amid laughter and more screams than anyone ever admitted, I'm sure, helped my mother shoo the bat out of the house.

When my mother returned the next summer, she found bats hidden all around the cabin, the result of a secret mission car-ried out by her friends. A rubber bat hung from the rafters by a stretchy string. A grinning cloth bat with orange stitching peered down from the top of a kitchen cabinet. In the bedroom a metal bat roosted on a windowsill. The bats are still there.

Although she feared bats, my mother loved birds. From the garden I would overhear her chatting with an eastern phoebe through the open window. She placed bluebird and purple martin houses in the backyard near bird feeders. After her morning run she scrubbed and filled the birdbaths, breaking thin sheets of ice from the surface on winter days, and filled glass hummingbird feeders with nectar all through the summer. Her high school biology teacher had taken students on weekend birding trips, letting them borrow his binoculars. He taught them to bird by ear too, something my mother carried with her. But, not surprisingly, no one taught her to love bats.

If she were here, I would take my mother to Bracken Cave and introduce her to the bats. We would walk the crushed granite trails and talk. Side by side, we would watch the bats emerge. I know that, like me, my mother would fall under the spell of the bats and the cave and the limestone landscape. She too would be surprised by the sound of fluttering wings, wild music that rises like a crescendo, filling the empty spaces.

Just before I start to head home from Bracken Cave, whispers of a storm swirl through the gathering. A quarter moon disappears behind low-lying clouds and all is still once again. I hurry to the car, using my phone's flashlight to find my way, stumbling over pieces of crumbling limestone. On a night like this, darkness is disorienting, at least for my human senses.

I roll down the car windows, imagining bat mothers nourishing their bodies with mouthfuls of moths, restoring the energy reserves necessary for mothering the same way I have tonight. I imagine young bats, their unsteady flight, listening for the reassuring flutter of their mother's wings nearby.

Following the rumble of thunder, a flash of lightning illuminates the purple-black sky. The backlit outline of storm clouds looks like the silhouette of a sandcastle city. And then silence. I notice the absence of fluttering bat wings, a sound I never knew before. I think of my mother, how I miss her fluttering wings.

I remember something one of the Master Naturalists shared. Her husband downloaded a weather app on his phone, a thermal imaging radar, and every night he announces the moment the Bracken bats emerge. The colony is extensive and produces heat, so much so that the bats appear as a red mass moving across the map. I plan to find that app. I plan to celebrate twilight, the time when bats emerge: a time to pause at the end of a busy day of mothering, to celebrate the strength, energy, and love of my own mother, and to settle into a newfound comfort that grows like a swirling vortex in the presence of wild bat mothers.

Soon bat mothers and their children will join bat fathers and migrate to Mexico to overwinter. They know the exact location of their winter cave, the shape of the entrance, the rough surface of the ceiling, the spot where the claws on their feet fit best. When they arrive, their tiny bodies will collapse from exhaustion, and they will seek shelter. By then bat babies will be strong enough to survive on their own. And in the spring bat daughters will find their way home again, to Bracken Cave.

I wish the bats well on their journey. I hope they will always find shelter—find home—in this world.

FALLING INTO THE SPACE ABOVE

I'd heard it said just birds could dwell so high
So I pretended to have wings for my arms
And took off in the air
— GENESIS, "MAD MAN MOON"

Once I believed the subterranean was the Hill Country's only secret landscape—a habitat full of cracks, crevices, and hidden creeks, where ghostly creatures like salamanders and spiders lived their entire lives in complete darkness, unseen. As ecologists and writers often do, I set out to uncover the web of connections, to unravel the threads of this limestone place known as karst—the place I now call home.

I lifted rocks and looked in holes and learned the names of plants and animals. On the rocky surface, I explored the edges of sinkholes, wandered through gorges, and traversed crumbling hillsides. Below the surface, I climbed down into caves, searched passageways for bats and crickets and harvestmen (aka daddy longlegs). I studied geology, how the intricate landscape—like a magical world sculpted from clay—formed from the comings and goings of ancient seas and the ongoing dissolution of limestone. Every new discovery, every new place, captivated me. But recently my perspective shifted. And when it did, things turned upside down.

"Maybe I can take you to see a bat tonight!"

I whipped my head around to see who had raised the possibility of bats. I had been kneeling on the ground with my son, Ryland, photographing a lone click beetle and a spider not much bigger than a comma—our first sightings of the night. Beneath the blinding porch light, the unlikely pair seemed disoriented, moving in slow motion, going nowhere.

Ryland and I headed over to join my husband on the far end of a covered patio, where a small group prepared for a late-night adventure: a full moon hike at the Westcave Outdoor Discovery Center near Austin. The illuminated porch stood out like a glowing planet, and a never-ending expanse of darkness just beyond stretched before us. Although I had visited before on an early fall morning, the nighttime landscape felt unfamiliar, like the doorway to an undiscovered universe.

Since signing up for the hike, I had anticipated the opportunity to catch a glimpse of the karst nightlife, an opportunity often overlooked. Ryland hoped to see a fox, my husband, Bryant, hoped to see a coyote, and I hoped for insects of all kinds. But bats had never crossed my mind. I assumed all thirty-three species of bats found in Texas had migrated or tucked themselves away to hibernate, huddled together, hanging upside down from remote cave ceilings. At that time of year, late December, bats seemed like something to look forward to, like wildflowers or caterpillars or bluebirds: those wondrous things that signaled the arrival of spring in Central Texas.

Bats had been on my mind for months, ever since I experienced my first bat emergence at Bracken Cave, a little more than an hour's drive south from the Discovery Center. From that night, I learned about the need for silence and stillness in my life. I learned to celebrate twilight and the importance of returning home. The more I read about bats, the more they became my teachers, like guides ushering me deeper into the mysterious world of karst. Living on Earth for millions of years, bats carried the stories of place on their wings. Little did I know that on that hike, I would learn even more from a mammal not much bigger than my palm, a microbat.

The bat comment, it turned out, came from a petite, animated young woman with glasses that seemed too big for her face and long auburn hair tucked under a sand-colored knit cap. Something about her energy reminded me of Ryland, as if she were my son in adult form. Lindsay was the education director at the Discovery Center. Her boyfriend and a colleague joined her for the hike. The volunteer guide, Amy, a woman close to my own age, rounded out our group of nocturnal explorers.

Lindsay shared that earlier in the afternoon, she had spotted a tricolored bat (*Perimyotis subflavus*) flying over the stream and heading toward Westcave. The unusual timing of the journey foreshadowed the arrival of a fast-moving cold front.

Unpredictable. It was the only word to describe the weather lately. Last winter, frigid temperatures that lasted more than a week resulted in massive die-offs and decimated local bat populations. The day before the hike, the thermometer peaked near eighty degrees, and earlier that day rain poured from dark low-lying clouds. As the sun set, the temperature plummeted more than forty degrees, leading to last-minute cancellations for the Full Moon Hike: first one family, then another, then another.

Even though our small group donned winter coats, mittens, hats, and sturdy footwear, Amy wrestled with one last detail— our destination. Would it be too cold? Would the rocky trail be too slippery? Should we stay closer to the building? The sudden blast of cold air had thrown everyone off . . . the insects, the bats, and the humans. When we stepped out from the covered patio and onto the trail, the thrill of something unexpected swirled around us in the spaces above and below.

Not long after heading into the night, a wrong turn led our group to an overlook—a platform that, in the darkness, extended into nothingness. Wind whipped across the land and rustled the sleepy, juniper forest, shattering the stillness. As usual, the rugged terrain pulled my gaze downward, as if guided by an internal compass. I peered over the edge of the cliff at moonlit boulders that toppled downhill toward the Pedernales River valley, out of sight. The wooden railing supported my body as I leaned into it, and my ears strained to hear the gurgle of water far below.

Soon I noticed Ryland shining his flashlight upward, searching for nocturnal creatures not on the ground, but in the treetops and in the sky. I followed his gaze. There, a break in the tangled branches revealed the Texas sky, as vast as the stories and songs promised. The full moon drifted into view for the first time.

Nearby Lindsay and Amy stared and pointed.

"Is that the Big Dipper over there?"

"I'm not sure. Wait. Yes, I think it is. I'm not sure."

"Well, I think that's the Little Dipper over there. Is that Orion's belt? Does anyone know their constellations?"

I shook my head; so did the others. In that moment I was painfully aware of how rare it was for the sky to enter my thoughts. After all, wasn't the sky as much a part of the landscape as the ground? For some, wasn't the sky an extension of home, as important as caves and creeks and treetops? Just as I had once been oblivious to the ecology of the world beneath my feet, now I wondered what had I been missing in the world overhead.

Later I learned that a new field of ecology, aeroecology, studies the diversity and behavior of life in the atmosphere closest to Earth's surface. The air is a place where a myriad of things take place: travel between habitats, foraging and feeding, and even mating. A multidisciplinary group of scientists monitors aspects of the aerosphere like wind currents, temperature, humidity, and turbulence. They study how these conditions affect winged creatures, wind-dispersed seeds, microorganisms, and fungal spores, all of the types of living things that depend on air, even the ones too small to see.

Scientists have found that human-made structures and conditions, like skyscrapers, aircraft, communication towers, air pollution, and light pollution, also affect life in the sky. Nocturnal aeroecologists specialize in the night sky, in the science of darkness and moonlight. Even thirty years ago, when I studied ecology in college, the sky was not a place people often thought of as home, but today it is undeniable.

I continued to stare up at the sky, as we all did, astonished by the enormity of it all. And there, in the moonlight, an idea took root: perhaps I had been looking down for too long, perhaps it was time to look up.

We stopped in front of a locked gate farther down the trail. Although I couldn't wait to see the surprise on Bryant and Ryland's faces, I already knew the secret that lay beyond: John Covert Watson Canyon Trail. Down a narrow winding set of 125 stone steps, surrounded on one side by a limestone ledge and on the other by a thick cable for balance, the trail descended into a canyon. For a while the trail meandered beside a cypress tree–lined stream, through an area of lush vegetation with fern-covered logs, and to a footbridge where cottonmouth snakes gather to mate and hunt in warmer weather. The trail ended at an enchanted place with a grotto (a large recess in a rock wall), a waterfall, and a cave—the very cave where Lindsay had seen the bat earlier that day.

After a quick word with Lindsay, instead of returning to the building, Amy turned and unlocked the gate. She decided to go for it, and soon we would be headed into bat territory. I gave a silent whoop. I stopped now and then, reminding myself to look up, to take in the sky.

About halfway down the stone steps, I realized that bringing my eight-year-old son on a quiet hike was not the best idea. After several gentle reminders that his loud voice might scare the animals, Ryland turned and stated in his most serious voice, "Mom, I'm having a conversation with Ms. Amy."

Kind and patient, Amy answered every question and even posed her own, encouraging my son to figure things out on his own as we hiked. She even showed Ryland how to shine his flashlight into the understory and find glowing spider eyes. In return, Ryland stopped frequently and abruptly to show us the harvestmen, some with long, slender legs and others with squat bodies and short legs, that scurried over his shoes. We crowded around piles of scat, one from a ringtail, a cousin of the raccoon, and another from a gray fox. Several moths flitted around my head, but mostly the night was still, too cold for fireflies or frog calls. Even the wind vanished. The shock of the sudden change in temperature brought a sense that, as we descended deeper and deeper into the canyon and the temperature continued to drop, the world had been frozen in time.

The week after the hike, a digital newsletter from the Hill Country Alliance, a conservation organization, popped up in my inbox. An article described efforts to preserve the Hill Country's dark skies. The area has experienced unprecedented population growth that continues to transform the landscape. Caves have been lost. Aquifers have been altered. And the skyscape has changed. As neighborhoods replaced ranches, city lights encroached. I am alarmed to find myself living on what many now recognize as the edge of darkness.

The article inspired me to delve deeper into the research on the effects of artificial light. When artificial light, especially LED lights, disrupts the darkness, it negatively impacts the lives of amphibians, insects, birds, mammals (including bats), and plants. It interferes with all aspects of the life cycle: foraging, sheltering, migrating, and mating.

For many living things, light draws them in and then leaves them disoriented. For others, the light repels them from certain areas, resulting in habitat loss. In Maine, near where I visit in the summer, frogs call less in brightly lit areas and froglets fail to thrive, growing much smaller on average. In England, moths lay fewer eggs in bright habitat and caterpillars refuse to feed. Migratory birds and bats and even some insects, like moths, butterflies, and grasshoppers, can no longer navigate, unable to find the moon and the stars, lost somewhere in the artificial glare. Insect populations, a resource bats and many other karst creatures rely on for survival, continue to decline.

Just past the bridge, our group settled onto rocks, with the grotto and the cave behind us. Amy told us about the history of the spot. Before it became conservation land in the early 1970s, people frequently snuck onto the private property and partied. It took volunteers a long time to remove all the trash—to give this place the time it needed to recover. And now it was protected. I felt lucky to be there with my family.

Amy challenged us to sit still and quiet for five minutes, a short time in reality but difficult for many. She asked us to listen. She asked us to pay attention to the light that trickled through the branches and made shadows that danced like rivers. It was like a scene in a black-and-white photograph with all the subtle colors in between. I began making a list of light words in my mind: dazzling, luminescent, mottled, resonant, gleaming, shimmering, striking, wavering, ghostly.

Having just visited Disney World, I began thinking about a new area on the grounds, Pandora, a recreation of the land in the movie *Avatar.* The engineered place, full of vines, gnarled and fern-covered trees, and rocky cliffs, captured the essence of a rainforest or a lush valley like this one. Without a doubt, it was spectacular, but it couldn't compare to this. It reminded me of the inability of humans to re-create nature, all of its complex relationships, especially the ones we don't know about yet. What will we do if these places—the rocky terrain and the dark skies above—disappear? What will happen to the bats and the harvestmen?

When the time ended, we all needed a moment to transition out of silence, as if we had lost ourselves in place, blended into the world around us, wandered off like wild animals. We took turns sharing our thoughts. Bryant was the first to share, something out of character for my sports-loving husband, the one who always seems to have a podcast making noise in the background. I leaned in to listen. The sound of the waterfall had mesmerized him. He thought about how old the water was and how long it had been flowing through the rocks. Then I noticed that Ryland lingered in that quiet space a little longer than the rest of us, looking upward. That, too, was rare and unexpected. I wanted to ask what he was thinking, but instead I gave him space to wonder.

"Let's talk about the bats."

Lindsay climbed on top of a rock. She was the kind of teacher and learner whose passion shone through at every turn. She couldn't hide it if she tried. She shared the natural history and ecology of the tricolored bat, the one she hoped to show us. A solitary, nonmigratory species, tricolored bats roost in tree cavities or rock crevices and consume insects, mostly moths, mosquitos, and beetles. When the weather gets too cold, they seek shelter in caves, where they enter a torpor state, a short period of dormancy, until conditions improve; their metabolism slows so that precious fat reserves are not wasted. They wait for change.

I took the opportunity to ask Lindsay about the discovery of new caves on the seventy-six-acre property, something I'd heard about from other visitors in the fall. She verified the stories and explained that in the past few years, several new caves had been uncovered along with several endangered species, like the Bee Cave harvestmen. The thought of more caves, more undiscovered subterranean places and creatures, sent a shiver through me.

"Shall we go?" Lindsay waved her hand in the direction of Westcave and began walking. Ryland and I jumped up to follow, untangling our legs like a pair of harvestmen bunched together on a cold night.

The steps up to the cave were slick, and a steady drip of water plunked down on us from the rocky ledges above. I stooped over, grabbing the railing near the entrance. The moonlight grew more and more distant, although it was not a deep cave. The path beneath my feet crunched. I had only taken a few steps when Lindsay whispered that she was going to turn on a tiny infrared light, one that wouldn't disturb resting bats. She surveyed the crack-laden ceiling.

"I see it! Right there! Look at that chicken nugget!" Lindsay's excitement burst into the enclosed space despite her hushed tone. We all rushed over.

As I looked, I held myself still, but in front of my face I sensed movement, like a silent flutter.

And then, although I couldn't see her, I heard Amy's soft voice. "I think there's another one in here, flying around."

"Where?" Lindsay said, a hint of concern in her voice. "There is! Quick, we need to get out of here!" Her concern was for the bat actively seeking a crevice to hide in. She didn't want us to interfere, to prevent the bat from finding shelter.

We made it back to the footbridge without incident despite the precarious conditions: slippery rocks, tricky footing. Rock. Water. Caves. Bats. And dark skies. Those things, all connecting the world below with the world above, painted a picture in my mind of what it meant to travel through karst at night.

That night, on the wings of bats, I found the space to breathe deeply, to take in not only the vast open space overhead but the darkness too, interrupted only by the moon and stars. How special, how rare it was to follow a bat through a disappearing landscape.

BENEATH THE
NIGHT SKY

It may have started on a winter hike, when I stood on a platform above a river staring at the moon through a tangle of bare
branches.

Or it may have started when I opened a link to "Twenty of the
Year's Best Landscape Photos" and an image filled my screen:
the silhouette of a lone human being, small, beneath the Milky
Way.

Or it may have started the night we took our Westie puppy
out for a walk, when my youngest, Ryland, stopped abruptly and
exclaimed, "Wow, Mom, look at all the stars up there!"

Those moments formed a collage in my memory, like snippets
of time viewed through a kaleidoscope—which event happened
first or in what order became irrelevant. Nestled in my mind, the
images flickered, illuminating the darkest corners at every turn:
as I drifted off to sleep or drove Ryland to school or cleared the
garden for springtime, making space for new growth. I clung to
those images, saw them as signs or clues (as I often do) meant to
stir things up, like a great gust of wind.

For the past few years my relationship with the Hill Country has evolved during treks into the limestone landscape, mostly
during fragments of time when my three sons were in school. I

have been a mother for nearly twenty years, and I learned quickly that if the boys (and their parents) were well fed and well rested, everything else would fall into place. My family grew accustomed to early evenings, snuggled in bed by eight p.m., leaving the nightscape for others to explore.

But lately events had been pointing me in a new direction, leading to a place I hadn't considered, one I barely had time to notice: the night sky. So, in the midst of my winter malaise, I shed layers of weariness and restless discontent and headed out into the darkness.

Like all living things, humans need the twenty-four-hour dark-light cycle not only to survive but to thrive and flourish. This cycle synchronizes aspects of our physical well-being, our mental health, and our behavior, collectively known as our circadian rhythms. Dana G. Smith, a science journalist who writes about the importance of protecting life's dark hours, reports that "every organ in the body abides by an internal clock."

Starting with our eyes, light and dark input is relayed to an area of the brain known as the hypothalamus, the master clock. This grouping of more than twenty thousand nerve cells orchestrates activities throughout the body, often kickstarting a series of biological processes: turning genes on and off, building and breaking down proteins, and stimulating and suppressing hormone production. Even in darkness, the body is a flurry of activity, a universe unto itself.

As scientists have learned, too much or too little darkness disrupts natural rhythms, causing humans to enter a state of desynchronization. Last year, as part of an experiment, a group of fifteen people were sealed in a French cave for forty days. Scientists monitored their sleep patterns, social interactions, behavioral changes, body temperature, heart rate, and other biometrics. Although an official report has not been released, participants described the experience as a time warp: they slept longer and longer each day, eventually losing track of time altogether.

Beginning in the 1960s, a French geologist, Michel Siffre, carried out three expeditions into caves to study the effects of complete darkness on the human body. After seven months, his longest expedition, Siffre described himself as unsettled, disoriented, and half-crazed; he even admitted having contemplated suicide. A team that descended belowground to evaluate Siffre discovered that he had developed problems with eyesight and memory, a loss of dexterity, and altered sleeping patterns, sleeping nearly fifteen hours every day.

Considering our modern lifestyle, it is actually the loss of darkness that threatens our health and well-being. Light pollution, characterized by excessive light from artificial sources like electronics or LED lights, interferes with the body's ability to sleep and rest. When exposed to prolonged periods of light, the body blocks the production of melatonin, the hormone responsible for making us feel sleepy. Because darkness is a critical time for healing and restoration, light pollution tampers with our metabolism, thyroid function, mood, and stress response. These disturbances can manifest themselves in the form of diseases like depression, obesity, and diabetes.

While science explains how darkness nurtures human health and well-being, recent experiences made me think there was something more, something less quantifiable—a deeper reason humans seek connections with the night sky.

A woven basket on my desk holds an entire universe. One by one, I pile paper planets in the palm of my hand, admiring their uniqueness. I place them on top of journals or next to stacks of books or near a mug of chamomile tea. Sometimes I rub the paper between my fingers while I think. Every time I sit down to write, a new universe appears: an unexpected arrangement.

The birth of the planets, a messy affair, unfolds atop my kitchen table. I have been doing this for years. The idea came from a You-Tube video. With her soft voice and alluring Eastern European accent, the multimedia artist Marta Lapkowska convinces me that I too can create something simple, something beautiful.

I tape down sheets of newsprint to protect the table's surface. With a stencil, I trace circles, usually five or six at a time, with a black Sharpie and cut them out from thick watercolor paper. Something about circles and swirls comforts me. They are something I can count on. I wet my brush and open the box of watercolors, unleashing the possibilities.

I choose ethereal colors first, wisps of starlight: buttercup yellow or apricot. On the paper circle, I paint a luminous band akin to the Milky Way across the middle. Working outward, I add dabs of bold color like midnight blue or deep purple. I have no talent, of that there is no question, but I have fallen in love with the supplies, the textures, the smells—the quiet ritual of it all. The kitchen table, covered in brushes and papers and paints, awakens my mind from the lull of a gray day.

Next I scatter droplets of water and watch them carry the paint away in streams. For a moment I sit with the unknown: where the paint will go, what new colors will emerge. This is my favorite part. As my eyes follow the streams, my mind follows suit and falls into a fluid state, free to wander. Sometimes the colors pool in a horrible mess; sometimes they reveal patterns—fascinating, even gorgeous.

This is how, without realizing it, I first fall in love with the universe.

I never imagined that the dark night sky might vanish. That space felt like a constant, like the rocky ground beneath my feet or my parents' presence in my life. Where I live, the skies are still dark enough to view the Milky Way, but change creeps closer by the day. I live in the second fastest-growing county in the United States, and changes to the land lead to changes in the sky. In places where explosive growth occurs, light pollution follows. Recently, in article about the city where I live, it was described as "the edge of night."

Many individuals and organizations are sounding the alarm, encouraging others to preserve the natural nightscape before it disappears. DarkSky International works to educate people about the importance of preserving the night sky for plants, wildlife, and humans. In Texas, many of the spots where I have traveled to learn about karst ecology have worked with DarkSky and received dark sky status, among them Enchanted Rock State Park, Devil's Sinkhole State Natural Area, and Lyndon B. Johnson State Historical Park.

Communities around the Hill Country, like Dripping Springs, are also working to preserve nighttime darkness. By passing outdoor lighting ordinances, communities can become designated as Dark Sky Communities. Dark sky compliant lighting uses amber/orange bulbs to more closely mimic natural light, like candlelight or the sunset. To decrease the area and distance light travels, shields are placed over outdoor lights to help direct light downward and prevent it from traveling into unnecessary spaces. These are examples of how easily change can be made to protect the darkness.

I began to plan trips to some of the Dark Sky Parks near my home, but I soon ran into roadblocks. Guadalupe State Park canceled an activity led by local astronomers due to high winds that could damage expensive telescopes. Enchanted Rock State Park canceled a stargazing party with a ranger due to near freezing temperatures. The observatory at Reimers Ranch shut down temporarily due to a COVID surge. Disappointment followed disappointment.

One day I shared this story with a group of writing friends, my growing frustration evident. As our conversation came to a close, someone offered a wise nudge, saying, "You may have to go on your own. You may have to go rogue."

As a small boy, Ryland stuck cartoonlike astronauts and rockets on his bedroom wall. Later he added lifelike planets with no rhyme or reason, mostly in spots he could touch. My husband, Bryant, climbed a ladder to place plastic glow-in-the-dark stars on the ceiling. The grandparents sent a night-light that projected the planets and, for Ryland's birthday, a clock that functioned as a mini-planetarium. He slept with the possibility of the universe swirling all around him.

Much to his delight, space was the theme of his kindergarten year. He chose a midnight blue backpack with planets and a matching lunch box and water bottle. At recital at year's end, dressed in a black polo shirt with glowing moons like polka dots, Ryland rocked from one foot to the other, hands stuffed in his pockets, and sang a solo about Venus, the gas giant. The words gushed too loud and too fast, and when he was done he raced to me, nearly knocking me over with an enormous hug.

Around the same time, my two older sons, Jackson and Keenan, stumbled into their own love of the cosmos: *The Planets*, an orchestral suite by English composer Gustav Holst. A favorite of the middle school band director, the music could soon be heard filling the quiet spaces of our home on a daily basis—the frantic twittering of the flutes, the intense entrance of the brass, the booming bass drum, and the calming call of the clarinets—an orchestra sweeping us away into the stardust and darkness of an unpredictable universe.

Keenan fell in love with the movement "Mars" because it was written to showcase the euphonium, his instrument—something unusual. Fast-paced, fiery, and tumultuous, the euphonium's brassy, celestial tones guided the listener to a mysterious place on a journey that sounded intense and urgent. Years later Keenan would play the solo in the high school performance of Holst's suite.

Jackson's favorite movement was "Uranus," which he still listens to often, especially driving back and forth to college. The work's lyrical style and slow progression drew him in, but in the end the twist was the best part. It came, he explained, when the music deceived the listener, leaving behind the quiet, contemplative moments and ending with a percussive full orchestra—again, something unexpected. Looking back, it surprised me how well the pieces captured not only the nature of the planets but also the personalities of my sons, as if planetary dust still swirled within them.

During Keenan's last year of middle school I chaperoned a band field trip. We traveled in a long line of yellow buses to listen to the San Antonio Symphony perform *The Planets*. On the way, the students were rowdy, excited to be off campus for the day. Reminders to sit down, stop throwing things, and watch their language set the tone for the trip. I spent most of the ride planning my escape. But much to my amazement, once the students settled into their seats and the music filled the concert hall, they fell silent under the spell of the universe.

"You may have to go rogue." Later that night those wise words lingered in the air and rattled my imagination. Before long, they would push me out the door, and finally I knew where to go: our land in Blanco. Purchased five years earlier, it had become a place of hope for our family, where we would put down roots, gather together, and strengthen our commitment to care for the land.

Although we lived many miles away, weekends were often spent exploring the thirty acres in search of caves or fossils or animal tracks, our way of introducing ourselves to the land and getting familiar with the cracks and crevices. Yet we had never stayed past sunset. It struck me as sad that we had missed the nocturnal landscape with all of its unique qualities. It felt similar to experiencing only one aspect of a friend, like a coworker you only see at the office.

In preparation for our expedition, I downloaded *Sky Tonight*, an app that promised to show us a map of the constellations and help us learn the stars by name. Every part of me believed a map would help me understand the universe and my place in it. And, like the stories told by the old mariners, I thought that recognizing the stars and their position in the sky would somehow help me to navigate unfamiliar territory.

After dinner Bryant, Ryland, Finn the puppy, and I piled into the car and drove northwest along two-lane country roads to Blanco, watching the suburban sprawl disappear in the rearview mirror. On the way through the center of town we passed a feedstore, a courthouse, a boot store, an antique store, and a barbecue restaurant. A few people strolled around the grassy square. As we continued on, the lights faded. Ranches popped up here and there along the road. Time slowed.

Our family land drops off from a hilltop into a juniper-filled canyon, spreads out into a shortgrass prairie, and ends near the edge of a dry creek bed. We parked the car along the side of the road and hiked to the top of the hill, arriving in time to see the sun set. Soon a handful of stars materialized in the cloudless sky, slowly at first and then exploding like fireworks. Were there hundreds of stars? Thousands? Other than a slight difference in size and brightness, the stars all looked the same. The thought of knowing them by name overwhelmed me.

When Ryland opened the stargazing app, the outline of a dragon, his favorite creature of the moment, appeared. The group of stars overhead was the Draco Constellation, Ryland announced. In early October we would be able to observe the Draconids, a meteor shower that happens when the Earth collides with interplanetary debris, creating streaks of light across the sky like a dragon spitting fire. I leaned over to Ryland and whispered, "When we live on the hill, the dragon will be watching over you."

It wasn't long before I caught myself being sucked into the mesmerizing content on the screen, forgetting to look up. When I finally did, three cell towers blinked red lights over and over, becoming more disorienting as the sky darkened.

Later I would hear a story from a neighbor. Several miles down the road, a man bought a rundown ranch and spent a lifetime restoring the land. He invited schoolchildren and landowners to visit and learn about land stewardship. He won lifetime achievement awards for his conservation work. Not too long ago, a new neighbor constructed an enormous tower nearby. Built to resemble a European landmark, it was meant to be a tourist destination, a place to drink wine and take in the 360-degree view. For the first time in fifty years, the man had to buy curtains for his bedroom window, to escape the tower's glaring lights as he slept.

From the top of the hill I could see miles in every direction across a terrain that dipped and soared, dotted in limestone hills. And there on the horizon to the south, I saw it, a hazy, dirty-yellow band: skyglow rising from the city. It seemed to ooze into the sky, a startling contrast to the surrounding darkness. I didn't expect to encounter light pollution miles from Austin that night. As the skyglow expands, light from the stars and moon will fade.

In the midnight hours, Rob Greebon climbed out of bed, loaded gear into his truck, and drove hours to a remote location in the Hill Country. He left his wife and daughters behind, asleep in their beds. Greebon is a landscape photographer, and he does this often. Many of his pieces capture the night sky: shooting stars, the moon in different phases, wildflowers under the stars.

I discovered his work as my fascination with the night sky and the Milky Way began to surface, while I was trying to figure out how and when and where I might be able to see it. Ever since that photo had popped up on my screen, I had the urge to stand beneath the Milky Way, as if the answers to all of my questions might be waiting there.

Greebon has a gallery titled "The Milky Way over Texas." We share a love for some of the same places. The first photograph of his I saw was *The Milky Way over Enchanted Rock*. Enchanted Rock is the place where I scattered my father's ashes. I remembered when he took me to the Palomar Observatory, an astronomical research center in California. I pictured my father climbing the granite hills of Enchanted Rock and gazing at the moon, and smiled to myself.

I imagined what it would be like traveling with Greebon, chasing the Milky Way and all the wonders of the night sky. His days are guided by the phase of the moon or the possibility of a meteor shower. He talks of the quiet solitude he finds while he works. He also acknowledges that in the future he may have to roam farther to find pristine nightscapes free of light pollution.

Ryland meandered over to the east-facing edge of the hill and plopped down in the freestanding hammock we had stashed on the edge of a stand of juniper trees. Bryant and I stood nearby in the grasses, our heads tilted upward. I glanced over at Ryland sunken in the hammock, phone resting on his stomach, legs crossed, eyes captivated by the blue glow. Had he actually looked up at the sky overhead? I wasn't sure.

For months I had thought we would need binoculars and telescopes and apps and experts to connect with the night sky. It occurred to me now that there would be a time and a place to learn the names of the stars, but not now, not here, with the sky overhead. I picked up the phone and returned it to my backpack. I told Ryland that without the glare of the screen, his eyes would adapt to the soft glow from the stars and he would see more than he ever thought possible.

Until then, I had also believed I needed to learn all I could and have a plan for everything. I needed to know names, both common and scientific, of the wildflowers, grasses, insects, birds—and I still believed it was important, most of the time. I had studied biology so that I could write about nature and know the facts. I had planned where to go to school and what life would look like. Before making big decisions, I had talked to my parents at length, gathering all the information I could, relying heavily on their experiences—so much so that I often wondered how I would navigate the world without them.

But there I was, without my parents, without a map. I exhaled a long deep breath into the chilly air. Then and there, I decided it was time to let myself wander and wonder without knowing what would come next.

Several weeks after stargazing in Blanco, Bryant, Ryland, and I took my in-laws to Wimberley Glassworks, a building with a hodgepodge of sunny yellow and emerald green walls located on the side of a rural ranch road. A friend had mentioned it years ago, but I had never found the time to visit.

Pearl-colored glass ribbons hung from the ceiling like enormous shimmering jellyfish tentacles. I walked straight to a far wall entirely covered in wavy glass circles the size of platters. The overlapping configuration gave the artwork a kaleidoscope effect that reminded me of the images of the night sky I had been holding in my mind.

Seated on wooden benches inside the studio with sweat trickling down our skin, we waited for the glassblowing demonstration to begin. Artist and owner Tim de Jong opened the glassworks nearly thirty years ago. That day he was making a gladiolus vase for a spring collection inspired by Hill Country wildflowers. The audience voted on the colors, grass green on the inside and deep purple on the outside, a combination that reminded me of my favorite flower, mystic spires salvia.

De Jong talked and worked, spinning a bullet-sized glob of sizzling molten glass on the end of a long, hollow pole. He paused to blow into the tube every now and then. When more color was needed, he rolled the glass into colored dust on a steel table. He worked quickly, efficiently. With his long arms, he twirled the pole clockwise in front of his body. The way he moved the pole reminded me of the marching band color guard twirling their flags to the rhythm of the music. Then De Jong reversed direction and the glass lengthened. Wavy edges formed at the vase's opening. In the final stages of creation he removed the vase from the pole with tongs, a tense moment, and, wearing Kevlar gloves, placed it in an apparatus designed to cool glass slowly.

De Jong's love for the Hill Country was apparent in the way he considered the impact of his business on the environment and community. He recycled broken glass shards. Using electric rather than gas ovens, he saved money and energy because he didn't have to heat the oven as high. He invited school groups to visit. He shared this story. He was from a high-achieving family who frowned upon his decision to pursue a career in the arts. But, he explained, "I would rather fail than be the guy who never tried to pursue his dreams."

There was something about him, just beneath his gruff exterior and cheesy jokes. He was a storyteller. I admired how, despite his wry sense of humor, he shared his vulnerability and passion with a group of strangers. He let us step into his creative process. I began to wonder if, as an artist, he had ever been inspired by the night skies.

After the demonstration I worked up the nerve to ask De Jong about the dark skies. With his sense of humor in check, he responded, "If I did that, it would just be black glass." Then he told me about a series he created called "Blue Aurora."

De Jong led me into the showroom and over to a grouping of three glass pieces about the size of milk cartons. Mostly black, the curvy pieces contained luminous copper and blue shapes like dripping starbursts. I asked De Jong how he created the starbursts, and after stating that it was a carefully guarded trade secret he hinted that it was all about chemical reactions that take place as a result of the high temperatures used to fuse glass. He said he used more chemistry and physics and math in his work than he could have ever imagined. He used waves as an example, pointing out how so many shapes in his glasswork naturally followed the pattern of waves.

The chemical reactions that created such magnificent movement in the black glass were not controlled. It was impossible. De Jong had to have faith in the unknown, that it would produce something unexpected, something spectacular. I realized that is often what the dark skies inspire in people, some sort of faith in the unknown, in the possibility.

As Bryant, Ryland, and I headed home from our night sky excursion to Blanco, another image sprang to mind. At the end of a late-night talk about the events of the past few years—the loss of grandparents, uncles, aunts, and the loneliness born of a pandemic—Keenan had held my gaze, paused, and blurted out, "There has to be something more after we die, right? There has to be."

In that moment, I froze. I didn't have an answer. I wasn't prepared. After all the loss and change our family had experienced, I didn't know where to begin.

But days after that brilliant starry night in Blanco, with Keenan's question still reverberating in the caverns of my mind, I took a walk, Finn trotting alongside. I stopped to look up at the moon, just as Ryland had reminded me to do not long ago. I imagined the waves of disturbance, the shifting layers, the unraveling of it all beginning to settle. In the healing presence of the night sky, I convinced myself it was possible.

I was ready to wade into the uncertainty, to go rogue in a world that stretched before me like that vast dark sky, mysterious and overwhelming. Perhaps along the way I would find answers to Keenan's question, or at least a place to begin: on a small hilltop in a dark corner of the world, beneath the moon and stars.

GHOST NOTES

1.

When illness claims my mother, crumbling landscapes comfort me. In these fragile places, lessons of disturbance and recovery manifest close to the surface. On hikes, I explore edges: the edge of a sinkhole or a gorge, a dry riverbed or a canyon, the base of a hill, shattered places where shards of rock protrude; places where old landscapes fade in the shadow of new growth.

Plants pop up from cracks in the limestone, their roots push through rubble, their petals display colors of salvaged sunshine. I take pictures, lots of pictures. I study plant names, both common and scientific. I delve into geology, learning the names of rock layers and fossils. After my mother slips away, caves call, a telltale whisper in my ear.

As I transition into a world without my mother, the rough edges of my life materialize. I twist and turn and go deeper. I descend into the subterranean in search of caves.

2.

My sons play instruments in the master bathroom. Tile floors. High ceilings. Space. These architectural elements make for excellent acoustics, the best in the house, they explain as they set up recording equipment and music stands. Sometimes they play duets, the trombone and the euphonium. They argue about who came in on the wrong count and never resolve the issue. More often, Jackson and Keenan take turns practicing, footsteps flowing in and out of the bathroom during the after school hours.

The older boys encourage their little brother to pick a brass instrument too. As a toddler, Ryland tells everyone he will play the tuba, but now the trumpet moves to the forefront. Four more years, and he will change his mind more times than I will remember. All three boys have long arms and fingers. They say their full lips form a perfect fit with the cupped mouthpiece.

Sometimes Jackson and Keenan play stand tunes or fight songs or melodies from a marching show. After football season, etudes, short compositions that focus on a particular skill, like scales, become daily routines, practiced over and over as they prepare for auditions. They play until the finger and slide positions meld into muscle memory; they play until the notes seep into the crevices of my mind. Sometimes the sound of something familiar fills the house, a holiday favorite or once, for an anniversary gift, our wedding song.

When my sons finish practicing, they fill the tub, bathe their instruments in warm water and dish soap. The euphonium resembles a nautilus, with curved piping that creates a shimmer under the water, like movement. The different shapes direct airflow and create sound: a brighter sound on the trombone, a darker melancholic sound on the euphonium. The boys reach for beach towels to dry their instruments, then polish them and oil the valves and slide. This attention to detail helps produce the most clear and beautiful sound.

Jackson and Keenan revel in the secret language of sound. Dinnertime conversation leads to "watch this" or "listen to this," followed by talk of favorite composers and upcoming concerts. Bryant and I both played instruments briefly, but it wasn't something we pursued. We glance at one another across the table and smile or roll our eyes just to tease the boys. We have grown accustomed to our sons' sly grins followed by "you wouldn't get it."

We can't imagine our house without music.

3.

En route to a cave, I spot a sign with the words "Ghost Note Brewing," an elegant black-and-white sign with words written between the lines of a music staff. Thick, blue-gray agave leaves spill over the sign's base. As I drive along rolling roads, my imagination fills with possibility: ghost notes, echoes; music that flows like water—sometimes a trickle, sometimes a torrent—over the surface, down into caves, and back again to the surface through springs; ancestral music; celebration and ritual; memories. Images flood my imagination, a story brewing.

Later I learn that a ghost note is more than a poetic image; it is an actual musical term. I spend an inordinate amount of time trying to understand the concept.

Several explanations:

"A ghost note . . . is a note that is played while muted. The result is a percussive rhythmic effect without pitch."
— everyguitarchord.com

"Ghost notes are musical notes with a rhythmic value, but without a recognizable pitch when played."
— lowentheoryclub.com

For help I turn to my son Keenan, who is taking a music theory class. Yes, he has heard of ghost notes, but he has trouble explaining the mysterious concept to me. It becomes clear that I would need to study the language of music in depth before entering into a serious conversation. Instead he points out that on a piece of sheet music, a ghost note is represented by an X—played but not heard, there but not there.

4.

When I write about caves, I listen to cello music. I can't recall how it started or why. In my mind, it is the music of karst—springs, sinkholes, underground rivers, and caves, the landscape of my home.

I come across an announcement for a concert series being held in the Cave without a Name, a favorite destination not far from my home. On a fall evening, a cello choir will play in the subterranean Throne Room, a cavernous space with spectacular natural acoustics. I purchase tickets right away, hoping my older boys will join me.

When I mention the concert, Keenan tells me the cello is the string relative of his instrument, the euphonium. I had never heard of the euphonium before he began playing six years ago. I learn quickly not to refer to the instrument as a "tiny tuba," although to my untrained eye that is what it resembles. The cello and the euphonium are the instruments most similar to the human voice, producing a sound that is expressive, haunting, dark, rich, and warm, Keenan says.

Suddenly I start to understand why cellos guide my writing: with their dark and haunting sounds, they ease me deeper into the cracks and crevices, the enigmatic spaces of the Earth's interior.

5.

What does the earth sound like? To answer this question Lotte Geeven, a Netherlands-based artist, records sound in a five-mile-deep hole in Germany. The project requires more than a simple microphone, which would quickly incinerate at thirty thousand feet below the surface. With the help of geologists and engineers, Geeven succeeds, although some speculate that the sound she captures is merely the clatter of the equipment.

Geeven describes the subterranean sound as similar to the rumble of thunder or the roar of a tornado. When I listen, I hear wildfire and wind.

She also discovers that people with visual impairments "hear" storms coming but not with their ears. Storms produce a low-frequency sound, a type of energy that human bodies sense in different ways. When storms approach or there is a noticeable change in energy, people with low vision report that the hairs on their arms stand up straight.

6.

In the hours leading up to a bat emergence, humans experience silence. Bats experience something altogether different. While the outside of the cave appears calm, inside bats scramble and jockey for position. They communicate constantly as they move closer to the entrance.

Bats communicate in a variety of ways, although most of their sounds are in the ultrasonic range, too high for humans to hear. Some bat species use high frequencies; others use low frequencies. And many are capable of changing their pitch. Scientists differentiate between species by the frequency, intensity, and duration of the call. While most bats produce sound using their larynx or their tongue, some species have noses that act as instruments.

Other than humans, bats have the most complex language of any mammal. Analysis of their vocalizations shows that they use sound to argue over food and sleeping position. They also intimidate intruders, recognize each other, and teach their offspring using sound. They use vocal sequences, like syllables, to produce meaning. The male Mexican free-tailed bat, for example, hangs upside down while singing a unique composition: a series of buzzes, trills, and chirps composed to attract mates—a wild love song.

While I wait to view a bat emergence, I learn that in the Hill Country, if humans could discern the call of millions of Mexican free-tailed bats during their nocturnal flight, the ultra-high-pitched sounds would be as loud as ambulance sirens. The ultrasonic call of little brown bats, a species known for its intense call, is louder than a smoke detector sounding next to a human ear. Unbeknownst to humans, the night sky is filled with sound.

Sound is there but not there.

7.

Belowground, scientists record and monitor seismic activity, waves of energy that travel through the earth's rocky layers like sound waves through air. At the surface and deep within the planet, they capture biological sounds—vibrations from earthquakes, underground explosions, landslides, volcanoes, and other natural processes. The energy released by ruptures, eruptions, and explosions forms patterns or rhythms. Scientists also capture the low frequency creaking and cracking of the earth's crust, the slow shifting of rock. They use this information to predict when and where natural disasters like earthquakes may occur.

Increasingly, human-made noise has been interfering with subterranean sound. Activities like road and rail traffic, airports, tunneling, construction, and quarry activity create a constant buzz.

But during the COVID-19 pandemic, the earth suddenly experiences quiet.

Human-induced seismic activity ceases . . . temporarily. Scientists hear the earth's sounds more clearly. Animals hear each other. Humans attempt to relearn the art of listening and communication. For many, when they hear their own inner rumblings in the distance, they experience discomfort.

8.

Hanna Tuulikki, a visual artist, composer, and performer, seeks out the hidden sounds of the "more-than-human world." In her work, she explores mnemonic topographies, unearthing the lore of places. She studies the way the land is encoded in song, and she believes human music grows from intimate relationships with the land.

Tuulikki incorporates the sounds of the natural world in her music. In her composition *100 Breaths, 100 Waves*, human inhalations and exhalations mimic the sea. She is also well known for her work with the musical rhythms of birds and seals, which she performs outdoors. She draws inspiration from keening songs, traditional Gaelic music sung to guide the recently departed through a portal to the spirit world. I envision Keenan's euphonium music guiding my mother.

With her current project Tuulikki hopes to incorporate bat sounds. She has put out a call for bat vocal recordings, ones that might include species from around the world. She plans to merge bat sounds with human music and dance, a model of "ecological coexistence."

At home I begin to carve out the mnemonic topography of karst terrain. I listen for wild music in my yard, especially during early morning walks with my puppy. While he digs in search of mice or fox or armadillos, the sun rises, shimmering on dew-laden leaves and grasses. I listen to the landscape and wonder, *what does karst sound like?*

In response to my question, sounds surface. I jot them down in my notebook. In the fall, the rustle of prairie goldenrod, seed heads swaying in the wind, provides the background for other music: the Cooper's hawk (*cak-cak-cak*) or the golden-fronted woodpecker, whose short repetitive squawks (*chuh-chuh-chuh*) sound like monkeys in the trees. On foggy winter mornings, the *drip-drip-drip* of water falling from branches and landing on leaf litter sounds like a steady heartbeat. The snuff and snort of a buck and the reverberations of his hoof stomping on the ground surprises me over and over again. I look forward to spring evenings when the deep-bellied croaks of toads drift from the creek. The sounds are as ever-changing as the seasons, the weather, the wind—like the movements of a musical composition.

Lately though, the whir of traffic becomes harder to ignore and drowns out the natural sounds. I often feel like I am missing something.

9.

While I'm visiting Natural Bridge Caverns, a series of caves and passageways near my home, the guide shuts off the lights. She asks the group of visitors to stay still and silent. Although this is something most people are unaccustomed to, it is something I have been craving. We are seated on narrow wooden benches in an enormous dome-shaped room. The air, damp and chilly, surrounds me and feels like the cave is breathing. The hairs on my arm stand up straight.

I sense that Ryland and Bryant are near, but I cannot hear or see them. I begin to wonder who else is nearby and what else I cannot hear. I think of my mother. Perhaps she is nearby too. Perhaps this is why I am here.

10.

Gordon Hempton, an acoustic ecologist, believes sound tells the story of place, and he has spent a lifetime listening. He has listened to migrating songbirds and the Amazon River and moss-covered fir trees and elk crashing through the forest, stomping on decomposing logs. He has listened from within a hollowed-out spruce stump and from a fern-covered forest floor and from the middle of a cornfield. He has recorded snow melting on mountaintops and the sound of waves from the beach. He has captured the symphony of dawn breaking across six continents.

Hempton's work inspires me to plan new places to listen to karst—next to a spring, within a sinkhole, on a limestone hilltop in the fog, from a gorge during a rainstorm. So many experiences await, new ways to know place.

Other scientists have discovered that human-made noise elevates caterpillar heart rates, interferes with bats' and owls' ability to capture prey, and increases production of stress hormones in elk and wolves. Birds, frogs, and bats alter their calls in response to human noise in order to survive. For humans, noise pollution has been linked to premature death and countless illnesses, like depression.

After years of research, Hempton is convinced that healthy soundscapes lead to healthy environments, that quiet benefits all living things. He founded Quiet Parks International, a nonprofit that works to preserve natural soundscapes. He begins by identifying pristine soundscapes and then works to preserve them. Through ecotourism, creating destinations similar to national parks, he hopes to produce the funds necessary to continue his conservation work.

As he travels around the planet, Hempton shares his vision for these protected places where people can listen to the rustle of leaves or birdsong or the trickle of streams. These places, he believes, are the "think tank of the soul." His work is about quiet landscapes, but he reminds people that quiet is not the absence of sound; rather, it is about the quieting of human-made noise—the clack and clang, the whine and whir—so that nature's music can be heard again.

II.

The night of the cello concert at Cave without a Name, the boys' busy schedules prevent them from joining me. Although I am disappointed, I am learning that this is something to expect moving forward as they dive into their own lives.

The crowd, dressed in a mishmash of skirts, scarves, heels, and hiking boots, winds across the lawn long before the concert begins. In line, two women, several years older than I am, set up a picnic on the ground in front of me. Until they ask me to take a picture, I feel like an intruder. They offer me a beer from their basket. They have been friends since their children were toddlers. They live hours apart but plan a special visit once a year. Their children are adults now with busy lives of their own. They sit stretched out on their sides on a flower-covered blanket and laugh loudly with the ease of old friends. In these two women, I see my future.

Not wanting to interfere with their time together, I pull out my phone and start to research cave acoustics. The size, shape, and condition of cave walls underground affect the sound produced. Long narrow tunnels generate echoes, and large rooms with domed ceilings, like cathedrals, produce prolonged sounds that resonate loud, clear, and deep.

When it comes to the location of ancient cave paintings, scientists have discovered that the most decorated areas are also the ones with the best acoustic response. These are places where sounds like stomping, clapping, and singing would be amplified, sounds that might bring art, like a stampede of bison, to life. Alongside paintings, instruments like vulture bone flutes, bull-roarers, and drums have been discovered. Sound and storytelling, ritual and ceremony exist together in subterranean spaces. Because of their musical quality, or aural architecture, caves have been used as sacred sites throughout human history.

12.

When Jackson leaves for college, the house falls silent. I follow the worn pathway in the carpet that leads to the bathroom, a space that feels empty without instrument cases and sheets of music scattered across the vanity. I listen for echoes, hoping sounds might linger, traces of my son held in the walls and the ceiling.

There but not there.

Keenan changes his routine. He plays his euphonium in his bedroom, where I cannot hear, or in one of the practice rooms at school. A few months later he meets with a new teacher who identifies a problem; he describes Keenan as a "bedroom player." His sound is diminished. During the lesson, his teacher runs around the band hall standing on chairs in various locations, yelling, "Louder, Keenan! Louder! More!" until Keenan feels his lungs cannot hold any more air.

Keenan returns home energized, his perspective altered. In an animated voice, with his hands flying this way and that, he tells stories over bowls of chicken and dumplings and then hurries to practice in the master bathroom. Before the next audition, his teacher reminds him, "Fill the room with your sound."

13.

In his book *The Longest Cave*, Roger W. Brucker, a Texas cave explorer, notes that "often you do not know where you are, but only where you started. . . . Cavers usually have to wait until their surveys are made into maps to know where they have been." During the holiday break I begin to put words on paper, to map my story. Like cavers and their maps, I only understand where I have been when I write.

I gather the boys, Bryant, and our Westie and head to Ghost Note Brewing, thrilled at the rare opportunity for all of us to be together. These days, arranging our schedules is no easy feat. Nearly a year has passed since I first saw the brewery sign, but the images have hovered just beyond my reach, a jumble of thoughts waiting to be sorted.

A message on the brewery website furthers my understanding of ghost notes: "Though seemingly unnoticed to the listener, [ghost notes] fill out the beat and add greater dimension and depth to the music."

Over drinks and snacks, our family talks about upcoming auditions and summer opportunities. Jackson will be gone the entire summer, touring with Drum Corps International. Trombones are excluded from most performances, so he learns to play the baritone, a marching version of the euphonium. Keenan helps, delighted to assume the role of teacher to his older brother. They sight-read holiday music together in the family room and fill the house with sound.

Bryant and I encourage our sons' love of music. We hope it will follow them into their adult lives, help them to navigate obstacles, in much the same way bats use sound to find their way.

In his book's introduction, Brucker writes, "What lures explorers to big caves is the possibility of discovering many miles of passages where no human being has ever been before."

I look across the picnic table at my three sons and my map reveals itself in more detail: the main passage branches off into the ever-expanding unknown. As I pursue unexplored tunnels and rooms, my sons, off living their own lives, will continue to add depth and dimension to my life, like ghost notes held in the cracks and crevices of ancient limestone.

14.

Twelve cellos, against the backdrop of a cratered limestone wall, begin their final song, "Hallelujah" by Leonard Cohen. The first note, played as a solo, causes the hairs on my arms to stand up straight. I experience chills as the music reverberates through the layers of my body in waves.

I watch the musicians' faces, many of them students around the same age as Jackson and Keenan. In shadows on the limestone wall, their bodies and their instruments become one; their arms, hands, and fingers move as if they are dancing. Some close their eyes. I do too, and sound rushes into the empty spaces of my body.

When I emerge from the cave, constellations illuminate the night sky. The transition from subsurface to surface is harsh: a change in temperature, in lighting, in sound. All at once the vast, wide open spaces aboveground seem too big, too empty, like all the music has been lost to the darkness. My mind struggles to adjust.

On the drive home, when familiar feelings creep in—the feeling of loss, the feeling that something is missing—I open my mind to the possibility of ghost notes echoing across the landscape unnoticed, like the softest breeze. I embrace the possibility that karst terrain, full of cracks and holes and empty spaces, can be filled with music, healing music, and the whisper of voices, wise and familiar, like my mother's: there but not there.

EMBRACING WHAT REMAINS

Several years ago I gathered a bit of wisdom, and from it I sketched a roadmap for the rest of my life. I was reading the essay "A Mother's Work" by Robin Wall Kimmerer, beloved mother, scientist, teacher, and writer. The wisdom, however, didn't come directly from her; it came from a book she had read by Paula Gunn Allen. For me, that shared wisdom transformed itself into something of a story, the kind passed from grandmother to mother to daughter.

Not long before I picked up Kimmerer's book, I began experiencing disturbances, small and sporadic at first and, later, like a flood washing away pieces of the past. I stumbled through unfamiliar terrain, missing my grandmother's guidance and clinging to the scattered pieces of my mother as she slipped away, losing her daily battle with dementia. Because of the expanding cracks in the ground beneath my feet, I received the gift of wisdom from Kimmerer and Allen with an eager heart.

This is the wisdom the two women shared: As a woman passes through the phases of life, her role changes—daughter, explorer of self, friend, wife or partner, perhaps mother. Eventually her circle expands outside of herself and her family. Her experience and knowledge grow, and she is called to tend to the well-being of the larger human community. Teacher. Role model. Keeper of stories and wisdom. And, as time passes and her circle continues to widen, something beyond the human community beckons. In the final phase, she embraces the whole planet and begins her work mothering the earth.

With the next phase of my own life fast approaching, I felt certain it would require a shift in focus, a restoration of purpose. My parents were aging, and my sons would soon leave home. Aunts, uncles, and cousins had died. My husband, Bryant, and I had experienced several health scares in the past few years, much earlier than I ever expected.

One morning, after weeding the garden, my back stiff and sore, I wondered to myself: *What would it look like, for me, to embrace a small place on this planet, to begin mothering the earth?*

On a drizzly December day, I carried my newfound wisdom to the top of a hill. Having read about a piece of land for sale in Central Texas, my husband and I went in search of a place to embark on our final phase.

We did a little research and learned that the land had been a ranch, mostly cattle and goats. Overgrazed and eroded, it offered plenty of opportunity for restoration projects. We were ready, having started with a tiny butterfly garden at our first house and moving up to a one-acre plot with native flowers, vines, and berry-filled shrubs. That day, our first meeting, we hoped the land would welcome us, that the hill would need us as much as we needed it.

After parking the car on the side of a narrow road, Bryant and I scrambled up a slippery hillside. Unprepared for the changing weather, I stepped into the fine mist wearing jeans and a short-sleeved shirt. Water droplets pooled on the surface of my skin and hair. The climb was less of a hike and more like maneuvering through a fogbound obstacle course made of loose rock. We weaved around the knee-high serrated leaves of spiky sotol plants scattered on crumbling limestone ledges. The air was still, the morning quiet. We stopped frequently to take in the view, or at least we tried. Instead, held in the fog's embrace, we came face to face with one another time and again. We kept on, confident that somewhere up ahead, obscured by a layer of thick stubborn fog, lay our future.

Three hours to ourselves stretched out before us, something rare. Our sons stayed at home, the two older boys keeping an eye on the youngest. As we climbed, my mind returned to the time when Bryant and I were just getting to know each other, wading waist-deep in a Utah river, part of a college biology course. The slick, algae-covered boulders and swift current had presented a challenge. How would we keep our backpacks from washing away? How would we stay reasonably dry and upright? Early on, we learned to rely on one another for balance and stability.

Over the years, our life together had expanded: three sons, four cats, one puppy. We had moved to a new state, and to new houses and new towns many times. We had a running joke, repeated in the car on the way to soccer games or birthday parties. We asked each other questions, back and forth: Can you believe we live in Texas? (We've been here twenty-one years now, in a place we originally moved to for one year. I'm pretty sure that is the biggest part of the joke.) Can you believe we have three boys? Can you believe our babies are nearly men? On and on it went, new questions always lengthening the list, much to our surprise. *Can you believe that someday it will be just us again,* I thought as we hiked up the hillside.

It didn't take long before Bryant and I reached the top of the hill. Worries flooded my mind. This place could be too windy. It could be too isolated. Digging a well might be an impossibility. It was far from the nearest grocery store. In the next fifteen years, with the population expected to double, it could be swallowed by sprawl. The school system might be too small. Maybe we should return to New England. On and on, the worries and doubts crept in. And then for a moment they trailed off. I knew they would return—they always did—but as I stood there, still and quiet in the presence of the fog-covered hill, the pause allowed the possibility to sink in . . . and the possibility of joy pushed aside the pile of worry.

Bryant and I left that day certain we had found our place.

When my parents die, I will fall apart. The sound of my own voice startled me. I had been carrying a sense of dread around for months, and, as a result, an unfortunate habit had developed: talking to myself out loud. Sometimes I could hide it, disguise it as a comment made to the cats or the dog. But not now, not in the stillness of the dark bedroom. It was as if my internal dialogue had bubbled to the surface and finally gushed out, as if my fears had nowhere left to go.

Crawling into bed, I couldn't tell if Bryant was still awake, if he had heard me. Selfishly, I hoped he had. I searched for his hand and found it, motionless between the sheet and blanket. I weaved my fingers into his and closed my eyes, willing my mind to slow down, to settle. I felt the layers of our family beginning to crumble and wash away with the passing of aunts, uncles, cousins. The silence shattered by the sound in my head, thoughts like waves crashing in, stirring up the stones along the shoreline. The rising rumble of tumbling rock—clank, clunk, crack—seemed to hang in the air.

Not wanting to disturb Bryant, I let go of his hand, moved to the edge of the bed. I turned onto one side and then the other. Then I heard it, a voice, sleepy but familiar: *I'll be here.*

Five years later Bryant and I returned to the hilltop with Ryland, our youngest son, on an early spring afternoon. Wildfire warnings and burn bans were in place, so we parked on the road again to avoid sparks that might ignite the grasses. We had promised the older boys we wouldn't move until they graduated from high school. We admired and encouraged their commitment to friends and activities, and so, although we visited the hill often, we waited to move.

At times it had felt like forever, the waiting. And then the time to move was less than a year away. Bryant and I had talked about restoring the land, but what would that actually look like?

That spring day we returned to the hill to meet with the Blue Heron Team, who would help us answer that question. After much searching I discovered them, a husband and wife named Scott and Colleen whose business motto was "Helping people to love their land." They had both worked on local ranches, helping with conservation efforts, for more than thirty years.

During my first phone conversation with Colleen, we quickly realized we had something in common; we were both environmental educators. It turned out we had something else in common; we had also both lost our mothers. I recognized a slight quiver in her voice, the sign of someone still reeling from the aftershocks of loss, still trying to find her footing in a world forever changed. As she shared her story, without hesitation, I felt we had both turned to the karst landscape of Central Texas to heal.

For Scott and Colleen, things began to fall apart during the COVID pandemic. Jobs had come and gone. A dispute over a will changed by an elderly man with dementia left them wondering if they would be able to stay in their home, a place they had been for the past twenty years. In the midst of turmoil, they decided to take an enormous risk and start their own business, the Blue Heron Group. In a short time they were contacted by a steady stream of neighbors. One woman wanted to create a place where visitors could come to view the solstice. Another neighbor wanted to make trails, and another wanted to restore a prairie.

I shared our goals with Colleen. We wanted to get to know the natural history and geology of the land, to make sure I hadn't missed anything. And we wanted to plan future restoration projects.

Colleen eased my worries about moving to the property, a swath of land that had been divided into pieces. She encouraged us to work with our neighbors to reconnect the pieces. Birds flying overhead would spot the green and hear the water, she reassured us, and they wouldn't care who it belonged to. Human boundaries were often inconsequential.

I was just moving through anyway. I would be temporary. And I was okay with that. That was enough.

Standing on the sparsely inhabited hilltop, I listened intently to Scott and Colleen as the wind gained momentum. I scanned the expanse of land before me, as if I could see the future, reel it in, and shape it just so.

Scott and Colleen's words revealed an origin story in my mind of how the hill came to be: Steel gray clouds moved in overhead, pushed by a wind that seemed to rush in unexpectedly from far away. After seasons of relentless drought, plump rain drops plummeted to the ground, making a thud upon impact. Then sheets of rain fell from the sky, the way it does during a Hill Country spring—passionately and without remorse.

Over time cattle and goats were introduced to the landscape. They gobbled up the greenery, leaving room for the swift moving water to carry away layers of soil, leaving the hilltop vulnerable. Deep water pathways, carved like scars into the land, dropped off over the edges. Layers of soil and loose rock washed away, leaving behind exposed bedrock. Again and again this happened, until the hill was all that remained.

According to Scott and Colleen, this is how to heal a disturbed hilltop.

"Think of the hill as a sponge," they said. If the water is given a chance to sink into the hilltop, it will fill the cracks and crevices and caverns within, feeding creeks and replenishing groundwater. The key is to slow down the water so it isn't lost, so it doesn't carry all the soil away with it.

Cut branches, lay them down on the hill, on the top and down the sloped surfaces. Decomposing plant material will turn to soil. Seeds will be trapped. Saplings will find their footing, and their roots will hold onto more water and more dirt. From there, everything else will follow—bacteria, fungus, insects, reptiles, birds, and mammals.

It is like tucking a small boy into bed, pulling up a favorite dinosaur blanket, or weaving my fingers together with my husband's: slowing down, settling in.

When you think about it, healing the land isn't that different from human healing, the way we adapt to disturbance. Slow down. Build memories from moments. Share stories. Protect them. Let them accumulate. Pass them on. Eventually the pieces, which were shaken or broken or scattered, will begin to settle. New things will grow from the cracks.

Near the end of our visit, my family, Scott, and Colleen crouched down near a steep drop-off. We peered over the edge. Fast-moving rainwater had deeply eroded a stretch of the slope, something that looked like a dry riverbed. At first it didn't seem like much. In fact, this type of topography was common there. I wondered why Scott had stopped at that spot. I knew there was a recess in the hillside, but it wasn't a cave, just an overhang. Scott inched his way down the steep terrain, ducking under a branch, lifting and stepping over pieces of dead wood and other debris. As he descended deeper into the eroded pathway, he grew smaller and smaller. He turned to the side of a bank above his head where a tiny madrone tree, several feet high, grew at an odd angle. Its rust-colored trunk caught his eye. He pointed to a pocket of soil at the base of the young tree and said, "This is promising, a sign of recovery."

It wasn't the first time I had heard that phrase during our time together. Earlier Colleen had identified curly clumps of grass that blanketed much of the lower levels of the hill. Seep muhly grass grew in moist areas, indicating that water was flowing below. Water, stored underground in aquifers, is something hopeful, a sign of recovery. In another area Colleen pointed out at least six other grass species like little bluestem and several early blooming wildflowers, a four-nerve daisy here and there, a cluster of blackfoot daisies. A diversity of grasses and plants emerges from a resilient ecosystem, another sign of recovery.

People's first instinct was to clear away dead branches, to clean up the land. Scott had to raise his voice just a little to tell the story as he was still making his way downhill away from us. Colleen, it turned out, had a bad knee that limited our exploration that day. Scott described the many times he had been called to tidy up an eroded waterway, but he urged us to let things be, especially in the canyon beneath the canopy of juniper and oak. Let the branches slow the flow of water. Leave the dead material to decompose in place and build new soil, just like on the hilltop. He encouraged us to embrace the messiness of the healing process and let things fall where they may.

The subtle signs of recovery hidden in the landscape took me by surprise. Small things I had missed, things I didn't even know to look for, were there all along. Given time, Scott assured us, they would lead to bigger and bigger changes, to healing.

I thanked Scott and Colleen for allowing me to see things from a new perspective. It helped to see recovery as a series of small steps, not only for the hill and the surrounding landscape but for myself. "Just give it time," I said aloud to myself from that point on.

"You may not see the changes in your lifetime," Scott remarked in his quiet way. Then he turned to Ryland and said, "But he will."

My mother has been gone for almost three years, my father for two. They both died in an instant—my mother from a stroke, my father from a heart attack. Despite my worries and attempts to prepare for the worst, there was little I could have done. My oldest son has gone to college, and his brother will soon follow. Ryland, the biggest surprise of all, will start fourth grade next fall. And Bryant has been here through it all, just as he promised.

Today our focus shifts to Bryant's family. He has to make a difficult phone call. He struggles to communicate with his mother, often running into a wall. Last week she was in a minor car accident, lost her balance on the stairs, and misplaced her checkbook, all within two days. This is how it goes now, the back-and-forth, the washing away, the building up, the starting over. And still we struggle to find our footing.

My phone dings. A text from Bryant appears: "Thanks for supporting me and being my rock." The next line mentions "friend rock" and "pirate rock," two excellent climbing rocks we visit every summer in Maine, named by our sons when they were young. "Not like those other rocks," he writes. "MY rock."

I think of the hill in Blanco, how it too is like that—the thing that holds us close and keeps us moving forward: OUR—the final destination on our roadmap.

THE UNRELENTING FORCE OF SMALL THINGS

Along a crack in the driveway, hordes of reddish-brown ants, hundreds at a time, appear as if from nowhere. Curious, I follow the ever-widening trail that moves through the yard like a river. The ants careen off into the beds of coralberry bushes, under the blades of inland sea oats, and up the thick, furrowed trunks of oak trees—vegetation I had carefully chosen and planted over the years. I add these observations to the long list of field notes from my yard.

On a path through the tall grasses, I observe ants covering cactus pads, climbing tree trunks, and invading bluebird nesting boxes. Each individual is no bigger than the print on a penny, but together their presence floods the landscape, like a miniature oil slick spreading out in waves. It is as if someone has opened a spigot, releasing a torrent of teeny six-legged bodies. Soon the hustle and bustle of the newcomers continues all day and into the night, week after week.

When it becomes apparent the ants are here to stay, I sit near the cracked concrete and watch, camera and notebook in hand. *Who are these ants,* I wonder, *and why does it feel like they are swallowing my yard?* They don't march in the orderly, single-file formation typical of other ant species. Although there is some semblance of a trail, many veer off from the group, as if pursued by a predator, like an antelope trying to elude a cheetah. Erratic. Frantic. Bizarre. On several occasions, I attempt to identify the ants using my iNaturalist app, but they are too small, too fast. The camera captures a smattering of vague, dark blobs.

As a biologist, at first I'm not concerned about the ant inundation. One of my ecology professors, an ant expert, reminded us often of their important role: ants spread seeds, aerate and add nutrients to the soil, and assist in the decomposition of dead insects and other plant and animal remains. Hymenoptera, the order ants belong to, is one of the most abundant insect orders, with a population of more than a quadrillion at any given time. Where I live, hundreds of ant species thrive. They have always been and will always be a part of the local ecosystem, but under normal circumstances they blend into the landscape, barely noticeable.

By midsummer unusual things crop up inside my house. Piles of ant carcasses accumulate along windowsills and in dark corners behind doors. After a vacation, the perimeter of the tile floor in my bathroom looks like a miniature mountain range. I sweep the floors, only to have the piles, inches deep, return overnight. Why these insects die en masse remains a mystery.

Outside things change too; things go missing. My wrists and ankles are free of fire ant bites, the clusters of bumps that itch and burn and look like pus-filled pimples—the telltale sign of a Texas gardener. This prompts me to scan the yard, searching for the familiar soccer ball–sized mounds, the fire ant nests, but they have disappeared too. At first, I interpret this as a victory.

I couldn't be more wrong. Days later I witness swarms of ants attacking grasshoppers, caterpillars, earthworms, and beetles. Under the passion vine, a fallen baby bird is devoured in less than a day. The buzz and whir and shuffle of life in the grasses—the comforting sounds of home—come to a standstill.

FIVE YEARS EARLIER

Balcones Canyonland Preserve, Austin

Not far from my home, scientists noticed swarms of ants climbing over their boots. As they rappelled down the craggy walls of a limestone cave, their headlamps illuminated millions of ants crawling in and out of every crack and crevice. They took note of their behavior, the way the insects darted randomly here and there. In contrast to the frantic ant activity, I imagine the unsettling quiet that descended as the realization spread.

Until that moment, Whirlpool Cave had been a success story. The city of Austin, multiple environmental organizations, and private citizens had come together to purchase and protect more than thirty thousand acres, including the fragile cave. A recent boom in development threatened several karst creatures of concern, among them cave salamanders and harvestmen. Now the karst landscape faced a new threat: invasive ants.

Although the scientific community had been dreading this moment, most citizens didn't see it coming. Exotic tawny crazy ants, native to South America, popped up in Texas and Florida in the early 2000s and have been moving west ever since. Because the queens lack wings, long-range spread is caused by human movement. Scientists believe the ants arrived in potting soil and took to the open roads aboard recreational vehicles.

Reports of ants ravaging local ecosystems began circulating, the list of offenses long: decimating crops, suffocating birds by clogging their nasal cavities, blinding rabbits with oozing acid, overtaking beehives, covering turtles' shells, knocking baby birds from their nests, and devouring scorpion and tarantula populations. It didn't take long before there was a marked decrease in the numbers and diversity of all other insects, making life for local birds, reptiles, and mammals a challenge too.

Being opportunistic nesters, populations of tawny crazy ants infested every possible preexisting crack, hole, and crevice, wet or

THE UNRELENTING FORCE OF SMALL THINGS   159

dry. Sinkholes and caves, prominent features of the cracked karst landscape, provided endless opportunity. Colonies also nested in rotting wood, loose soil and bark, and cans and buckets, and under rocks. They were even discovered living inside the bones of human remains.

Fierce warriors, crazy ants steal venom (formic acid) from fire ant abdomens, turn around, and use it against its maker. They form interconnected amoeba-like super colonies, with hundreds of queens capable of rapid reproduction. Words associated with crazy ants: Outcompete. Displace. Monopolize. Alter. Devastate. Wreak havoc. Annihilate. Their arrival is never good news.

That day at Whirlpool Cave, huddled in near darkness, the scientists continued their survey despite the presence of ants. (The ants' venom is not noticeable to humans.) They recorded the presence of other cave dwellers: salamanders, harvestmen, cave crickets. Still no bats, but for now that was okay. Clinging upside down from the cave ceiling, asleep, tiny bat bodies are vulnerable to ants. The scientists left the cave with the understanding that things had changed. Their job shifted from monitoring ecosystem health to studying the impact of the tawny crazy ant population on the cave over time.

Not long after, in areas of severe inundation, scientists began describing something unimaginable—an unnatural silence: A loss of insect noise. A loss of bird song.

Losses, both small and big, spread over the karst terrain.

FIELD NOTES FROM WITHIN

There comes a time, after so much has happened, when it is necessary to take a look around, take inventory, survey the damage. With their notebooks and computers, scientists head into the field. This usually follows a natural disturbance—a flood, a freeze, a wildfire, a drought, an invasion of exotic species . . . or a pandemic.

For me, this happened as the trauma of the COVID-19 pandemic waned after many years of loss and disturbance—the kind that alters a life the way natural disturbances alter a landscape. Balancing close to the edge, I willed myself to take the plunge, and then, cautiously, I entered the darkest corners of myself.

At first I assessed all that was, the big losses, the series of interconnected voids: the death of my aunt and uncle from cancer, my mother's battle with dementia, my father-in-law's death, my mother's death from a stroke, my father's death from a heart attack. All of these events happened over the span of seven years.

I marked them on the map easily, big and bold. These were the losses easily observed and acknowledged, their impact over time undeniable.

FIELD NOTES FROM MY YARD

Several months later, while I am writing on the front porch, the crack of a twig causes me to glance up from my work. A new neighbor stands at a distance, partially obscured by a persimmon tree. Unsure if she is keeping her distance because of the pandemic, the fear of spreading a virus, or some other reason, I stay seated.

Parting a branch to make eye contact, she blurts out, "Are you having trouble with ants?"

The question, along with the woman's stern tone, catches me off guard, almost like an accusation. I shift into defensive mode. I am accustomed to being at odds with my neighbors about wildlife, especially insects and snakes. I am a wildlife gardener. I plant native plants for pollinators. I leave piles of twigs and dead grass for birds and small mammals to burrow and hide in. I leave unraked leaves for overwintering caterpillars. I place rocks for reptiles to sun themselves. I avoid pesticides. My neighbors in the back continuously offer to mow for us but, for me, wild yards hold possibilities.

"Yes! There seem to be way more than usual." I say, and smile, trying to be friendly and open to conversation.

"They are crazy ants, you know. They will get into your electrical boxes and your air-conditioning unit and your septic system and cause thousands of dollars' worth of damage. I called pest control. I'll send them over when they finish here."

I wonder if she thinks my yard is the cause or, even worse, the hotspot of the ant infestation.

After a few more brief, uncomfortable exchanges, she turns and walks away, disappearing as quickly as she appeared, like an apparition delivering a dire warning.

I pack up my books and laptop and head out on a hike to avoid the knock at the door—the dreaded arrival of the pest control people. As the ragged books on my bookshelf will attest, I carry the lessons of Rachel Carson in my heart. My house sits within the Edwards Aquifer recharge zone, an area close to the surface where rainwater travels down through the voids and limestone channels deep below. I feel I have a great responsibility to prevent pesticides and herbicides from making their way into the subterranean streams and pools.

But the ants remain on my mind, so after dinner I rummage around our nature table until I spot a bug box hidden beneath feathers, rocks, and pieces of a cicada exoskeleton. I send my son to the driveway to capture an ant while I pull up a detailed photo of the crazy ant (*Nylanderia fulva*) on my phone. With a specimen secured in the plastic box, I stare through the fingernail-sized magnifying glass on the lid. The speck transforms into a living being with alienlike antenna waving wildly.

After comparing the ant to the picture on my phone, I pass the box to my son and let out a long breath. "There," I tell him. "See those long legs, those extra-long antennae, that tawny-colored body?" Check. Check. Check. The characteristics match.

My neighbor was right. Tawny crazy ants have invaded our one-acre yard.

I think of all of the plants and animals I have documented and photographed in my yard, nearly 350 species in the past few years. The joy. The excitement. The beauty. The peace. Wildlife gardening fills me with hope and purpose and love and a tangible connection to something greater. I cling to the idea that I have created something special, a small-scale restoration. A sanctuary. Yet sadness and a sense of loss settle in alongside the ants.

FIELD NOTES FROM WITHIN

Near the voids, I stumbled onto the faint trails of smaller things, the cracks, the things that piled up when I was overwhelmed: my son leaving for college, my mysterious and long-drawn-out anemia diagnosis, the sale of my childhood home, my mother-in-law's move to a care facility, my husband's blood clot, my third son's ADHD diagnosis, the slow drip of my new writing project, the delay of our move to Blanco, my special place. One after the other, they formed crumbling layers, the walls of an unstable subterranean space.

Before moving on, I marked those places on my map too. Subtle. Shadowy. Easily overlooked or dismissed. I remembered thinking, *The world is experiencing enormous loss and change. We all feel lost. It could be worse. These things are small. They will pass.*

But here they are, carved into my body, their impact over time unknowable.

RESEARCH NOTES

I launch into research mode and read as much as I can find about crazy ants, which isn't much. All articles lead to one scientist, Ed LeBrun, who works at the University of Texas. He runs the Invasive Species Research Group at the Brackenridge Field Lab and has been studying crazy ants for decades. He is the go-to guy, the key to saving my yard.

In 2015 LeBrun had a breakthrough. His previous studies found that the usual methods for ant control, like bait, were ineffective. One day he encountered wild crazy ants under the microscope with an unusual trait: enormous bloated intestines. Following dissection, he isolated a funguslike spore that commandeered the ants' digestive systems. The spore seized fat cells and reproduced rapidly, eventually killing the ant. Upon further investigation, LeBrun witnessed worker ants transmitting the spores to larvae. The disease spread like a virus, and the density of the colony declined.

LeBrun's team decided to experiment in the field, to see if they could spread the disease to other wild tawny crazy ant populations in infested areas. Using hot dogs as bait, they commingled infected ants with healthy ants. Soon the infection spread through the densely populated super colonies.

Whirlpool Cave was one of the experimental sites. The pathogen was introduced in spring 2017, not long after scientists discovered the ant population crawling over their boots and up and down cave walls. Two years later the ants were almost completely eliminated from the site. Even better, the pathogen did not appear to affect other insects or wildlife. Now it is considered to be a natural and sustainable form of biocontrol.

Unfortunately, spreading the pathogen is an expensive and time-consuming investment, according to LeBrun, and it will not be readily available to homeowners anytime soon. As the ant population in my yard explodes, I find myself running out of ideas.

FIELD NOTES FROM MY YARD

Months pass and temperatures drop. The ants retreat underground, I learn, where they will spend the winter. Activity shifts from the surface to the other world, the hidden one beneath our feet, where all that happens is not readily seen or easily understood.

I go to sleep imagining ants all around, traveling aboveground, belowground, in all of the nooks and crannies in between. Eventually I tuck my worries away, into the dark caverns of my mind.

I barely think of the ants again until Halloween. My youngest son decides to be Ant Man, not because he has any particular interest in bugs or the superhero but because he wants to help out a friend who can't decide whether to be Ant Man or the Hulk. The solution: they will divvy up the costumes and trick-or-treat together.

After meeting up with friends, we visit a few houses in our neighborhood. About five houses down the street, two older couples, neighbors and friends it turns out, sit in lawn chairs, holding glasses of wine, a plastic cauldron of treats set out before them.

One of the men waves us over. "And who are you? Spiderman?" My son explains his costume, sharing the story of the dilemma. "At least he's not a fire ant, right?" I say, and laugh.

"Or a crazy ant," he responds.

I open my mouth to say something else and stop as his words hit me. "Do you have crazy ants in your yard?"

He shakes his head and says, "We *had* crazy ants in our yard. What a nightmare."

My neighbor embarks on a story. The details are familiar— piles of ants everywhere, trails of ants through the yard and up the trees. They used ant bait and pesticide treatments. After two years, they are ant-free. Part of me is relieved. My wild yard was not the hotspot after all.

I can't help but ask the couple, "Didn't the pesticide kill everything else in your yard too?" I think about the butterflies, the praying mantis, the spiny lizards safe in the bushes near my house. From the neighbor's jumbled response, I'm not sure this was something they considered, or perhaps it was of no concern. I can't be certain.

As I say goodbye, my neighbor leaves me with some words of advice. "Take out your phone. Put this name and number in there and make sure to call Mike and his wife. They own the pest control company; they know what to do."

As usual, I hold out. I wait.

FIELD NOTES FROM WITHIN

This is an experience I carried with me down through the layers and winding tunnels.

Not long ago a friend suggested I listen to an episode of the *Ologies* science podcast, "Death, Grief, and Mourning" with Cole Imperi. After dropping my son at school, I hit play and settled into the driver's seat of my car. In the episode, Imperi explained that she is a thanatologist, a person who studies death and the process of grief. Not only does she assist those who are dying, but she also aids in the grieving process for the living. She points out that most Americans are not prepared for either experience.

Halfway through the episode, something grabbed hold of my attention. I had to pull over. I had to go back and take notes. Imperi shared her ideas about "shadowloss," a concept she coined. She described shadowloss as an experience of loss: "A loss *in* life, not a loss *of* life." Examples of shadowloss include things like missing out on a job opportunity, not attending a graduation, an estrangement, or a divorce—experiences that accumulated for many people during the COVID pandemic.

Imperi urged listeners to acknowledge those feeling of loss, however small they appeared at first. She created circular purple pins that read, "I'm grieving. Be kind. Be gentle," and delivered them to those in need.

I was reminded of my experiences, the small ones I had tried to sweep away and bury. The ones I accepted as part of life and moved on quickly from because at the time there were so many.

I decided to revisit those places, retrace my steps on the map. And there it was, a big one I had missed, hidden amid the unstable layers. After my father's death, during the height of the pandemic, I put off his celebration of life. I told myself I would get to it when things were better, but I never did. I put off the grief and mourning, waiting for things to pass.

FIELD NOTES FROM MY YARD

By the following spring, one year after the crazy ants' arrival in my yard, another change occurs, one I can't ignore or sweep away: ant trails zigzag across the kitchen counters, much too close to my son's frozen waffles. When I open the windows, ants tumble out. My teenage son finds them crawling along his bedframe near the window. My husband finds them in the shower. When the internet goes on the fritz, we envision ants in the wires and walls. My cat hovers over a trail weaving through the carpet, where ants teeter on the tops of fibers like unprepared climbers ascending the summit of Mount Everest. We are no longer facing piles of dead individuals but live ants invading our spaces, clambering over dead ant bodies piled along the edges.

In the past my family has put up with my peculiar passions without complaint. When baby geckos wandered into my son's room we captured them in containers and released them. When there was a tree toad in the bathtub, a giant centipede on the couch, and a scorpion with babies on its back in someone's sock drawer, we released them. All of my family members have a story like this to tell, but they reach their limit when the ants arrive.

I feel defeated. I worry about the wildlife, the other mothers and their babies who call my yard home. I welcomed them into our shared space, and now that space poses a threat. It is time to call Mike.

After briefly inspecting my yard on his way to the front door, Mike greets me with a harsh observation: "I'm not going to lie. What you've done here is create the perfect habitat for crazy ants."

Stepping over an ant-filled crack where the walkway meets the front porch, he points out the little human-made creek, the inland sea oats, arching, heavy with seeds, along the house's front perimeter, the thick layer of leaf litter under the oaks. Water. Food. Shelter.

Had that phrase come out any other way—perfect habitat for caterpillars, perfect habitat for migrating birds, perfect habitat for dragonflies—I would have hugged Mike. Instead I fall silent. I listen. Given what I know about LeBrun's research, I'm not optimistic, but I am curious to know if Mike has any new information to offer, some saving grace.

He explains that the pesticide, or bait, if applied regularly, temporarily pushes the ants away, but they return before you know it. Ineffective, just as LeBrun found. I imagine that my neighbors' ants fled their yards and headed directly to mine. In my case though, Mike doesn't believe he can access the perimeter of the house effectively. He refuses to waste my money returning time and again. I appreciate his honesty.

Mike's suggestion: Cut everything to the ground. Tear out the inland sea oats and the salvia. Haul away the leaf litter and the mulch. Clear out the piles of sticks. Turn off the water source. Remove the rocks from the perimeter. Tear it all down. But even then, he can't make any promises.

The scene that grows in my imagination is one of an apocalyptic landscape. Was it possible that everything I thought I was doing right was wrong? Instead of an oasis, had I created a hellhole? Still, I'm not ready to tear it down. I'm not ready to begin again, not yet.

Before leaving, Mike offers one last thought, "Eventually the ants will eat their way through here and move on." Then he shrugs, apologizes again, heads to his pickup truck, and drives away.

In the wake of Mike's visit, I do the only thing I feel capable of. I step back; I wait—but for how long? Sometimes I think the waiting requires more patience than I possess. I am waiting, waiting, always waiting . . . for something else to happen, to grieve for the loss of it all.

ADRIFT

Layer by layer, story by story, we build the self from scars and calluses.
— KEN LIU

After my parent's ashes had drifted into the bay, a long stillness ensued. I waited and waited for things to settle. Then one day I felt the pulse of something passing through, something not yet visible. I pursued it the way a child might chase a firefly in the darkest meadow, zigzagging this way and that, no path, no plan. Although familiar, the feeling—a certain kind of longing—had been elusive, waiting tentatively to emerge from the rubble of the past few years.

To understand that feeling, my brain poked and prodded and eventually pushed my body through the open door. It was just like me: in the midst of unimaginable change, I craved stability; in the midst of stability, I craved unimaginable change. Dichotomies like that have lurked just below the surface all my life, something akin to restlessness.

An online notification for a kayak tour of Spring Lake popped up. I reserved a spot immediately. During the COVID-19 pandemic, lake exploration, along with so many other things, had come to a standstill. The opportunity signaled the possibility of something new.

Years earlier I had been introduced to the lake aboard a glass-bottom boat, part of an educational program sponsored by Texas State University and the Meadows Center for Water and the Environment. After that I never missed the chance to take visiting friends and family on the boat tour.

When my youngest son turned four, we celebrated his birthday aboard one of the old boats, a remnant from the 1940s. The children circled around a rickety railing, peering through the glass into the crystal-clear depths below. They hooted and hollered when an alligator gar, with its elongated snout and ancient eel-like body, revealed itself, cruising through the blades of submerged aquatic grasses like a phantom.

One day several years ago, I packed up my writing and spread out on the lake's grassy banks. Before leaving, I ducked into the tiny aquarium. No one else was there. Dark and cool, the environment inside captured the feeling of an underwater cave. In tanks, ghostly white Texas blind salamanders wedged themselves into the porous limestone walls. In the wild, the slender, long-limbed salamanders lived belowground in the conduits of the aquifer. Other tanks held different salamander species, like the San Marcos salamander. A dark reddish-brown, these salamanders possessed more shadowy forms. They lived aboveground near the springs, feeding on algae, aquatic insects, and snails. Rarely seen, the salamanders of Spring Lake tucked themselves away like a secret.

Despite the thrill of those experiences, I had never kayaked the lake. Access is limited because of the lake's conservation status. You can't show up with a personal kayak and launch from the banks, for example. Threatened and endangered species like the San Marcos salamander, Texas wild rice, and the fountain darter, a tiny olive-colored fish with black splotches, relied on the springs for survival. These species and others throughout the area were endemic, found nowhere on earth except the unique spring-fed ecosystems of Central Texas.

The San Marcos Springs, made up of more than two hundred underwater springs, have been continuously pumping clear, cool freshwater from the aquifer, connecting the watery world below to the world above. Long ago the springs burst from a shallow river, breaking the surface and spraying water high into the air, but after the San Marcos River was dammed in the mid-1800s a lake formed and the springs were submerged. The cratered undersurface of Spring Lake resembled a skin, a thin and fractured boundary where two worlds touched.

Throughout time and through different eyes, unexpected and sometimes unimaginable things drifted through the enormous cracks. Spring Lake and the surrounding area has been the longest continuously inhabited site in North America, according to archaeological records. For local Native Americans, it had been identified as their place of origin. This is the Coahuiltecan creation story tribal member Maria Rocha told aloud:

A long, long time ago there was an Upper World and a Lower World. In the Upper World were all the things of Mother Earth—the trees, the hills, the animals, the birds, everything except the people. At that time the people were spirits in the Under World. But one day an entity took off her head and threw it into the sky. And it became the moon. So then the moon started having an effect on the earth and that effect was so powerful that it reached into the Lower World, and all of a sudden the spirits became people. But they were in the Under World and somehow had to get up onto the Upper World where Mother Earth was. The people prayed and a deer appeared to them, and the deer led them through the Under World. They went through rocks and crevices and mud and earth and all kinds of obstacles until they came to a portal where up above them was full of water. The deer started swimming up through the portal; so the people grabbed onto the deer and the deer grabbed onto the people. They were swimming and swimming up through the portal. At the same time there was a water bird flying over the springs. The water bird dove into the water and pulled the deer and pulled the people up onto the shores of Mother Earth. And that is how the people came to be on earth. We believe that portal, that crevice, was the headwaters of the San Marcos River, which we call the Sacred Springs. We believe that is our creation site because it is documented on a four-thousand-year-old rock art painting.

As I had learned many times in my exploration of karst terrain, a place full of cracks was a place full of possibility. With that idea swimming near the surface of my mind, I arrived early on a fall morning for the kayak tour. I meandered down the cedar-lined trail toward the lake, feeling welcomed by the trees and the water. In their presence I felt settled, if only for a moment.

Along the way I encountered two young woman, hand in hand, dressed in Texas T-shirts and swim shorts. One of the shirts caught my attention: a mermaid swam across it. I complimented the woman on her shirt, and she proceeded to tell me about the San Marcos Mermaid Society. The group led stewardship projects, like removing trash from the riverbanks, and organized educational outreach projects. She urged me to join. The prospect of becoming a freshwater mermaid captured my imagination.

The women also shared the story of the ancient cedar trees. Each tree was between three hundred and four hundred years old. For years they stood alongside a parking lot, but the area had been rewilded. For as far as the eye could see, inland sea oats, a native grass, and the watermelon red flowers of sleeping hibiscus surrounded the trees' massive trunks. After all that time, the trees, like water guardians themselves, had been protected. I sensed a certain wisdom swirling around me, through the rocks and the water and through the mermaids who returned to care for it.

At the water's edge a handful of people gathered near neon-colored kayaks lying side by side in the grass. Following a safety talk, our guides described the wildlife we might see, which included shorebirds and turtles, fish and dragonflies. One of the young women I had met smiled and, with a mischievous twinkle in her eye, whispered, "Or maybe mermaids."

Even though I had visited the lake many times, pushing off into calm waters that morning felt like gliding through a door into another realm. Soon I would understand why. Despite years spent getting to know the karst landscape, its sinkholes, caves, springs, and disappearing streams, I never knew what swam unseen through the waters of Spring Lake.

On my first day of life, I was set adrift. My origin story, written in the form of a poem years later, described a tumultuous saltwater journey. I tumbled and traveled with the currents like so many free-floating, glasslike larva. Eventually I washed ashore along the Maine coast, where my father scooped me up and carried me home. That was the story I imagined, the story I chose to tell myself.

Of course, the legal documents told a different story. My adoption took place in a California courthouse in the early seventies. My birth parents lacked the resources to care for me, I was told. The young couple, teenagers at the time, signed the papers and released me.

When one's DNA is a mystery, anything seems possible, and as a little girl I imagined my own metamorphosis. At night I transformed into a mermaid and dove below the surface, swimming with the plants and animals who lived in the deepest, darkest places—the places off-limits to humans. In my dreams, I returned home to my family in the sea.

For the longest time, the idea of having two forms, like a mermaid, intrigued me, and despite some of the not-so-nice attributes of the mythical sea creature, the ability to pass back and forth between realms seemed like the ultimate lifestyle.

As I grew, I set my more mature and realistic sights on becoming a marine biologist. In college I enrolled in all the saltwater courses offered, studying everything from seaweed to sea stars. One winter I lifted barnacle-covered rocks and collected data on juvenile lobster populations living in the intertidal zone. The next summer I donned hip waders, and from knee-deep in the mudflats I collected, counted, and measured marine worms. For my thesis, I examined the roots of salt marsh grasses, assessing the overall health and well-being of the marsh, a place where salt water and fresh water merged. The summer after college, I worked for the Whale Conservation Institute. I spent my days at sea documenting whale behavior and migration—the ancient journey of the humpback whales.

Each field experience presented a chance to pass through a new world, if only for a moment. In those places, stories presented themselves, and I gathered words and images, letting them settle into the cracks and crevices of my body.

During that summer I also learned that because of my asthma, scuba diving was off-limits. Getting to explore the underwater world was a dream I would have to abandon. And so, tethered to the deck of a boat, I scanned fog banks and strained my ears for the startling and explosive exhale: the blow of a whale. Every time a whale broke the surface, I caught a glimpse of the mysterious life below. My lifelong fascination with hidden worlds grew stronger year by year, story by story.

The tranquil waters along with the soft morning light created the perfect conditions to kayak Spring Lake. Leaning over the edge of the kayak, I could see far, far below. I paddled from place to place, following the tangled threads of an ever-evolving story: the relationship between people and a special place.

Not long ago, people traveled from miles around to see mermaids swim in Spring Lake. The story began in the 1920s when the lake and surrounding land were purchased by the owner of a local coffin store. He built a hotel and later offered glass-bottom boat tours.

In the 1950s the owner's son acquired the property and grew the attraction. One of the men on our tour had worked at the lakeside concession stand as a teenager. As our kayaks gently clunked together near the old hotel building, he shared a first-hand account of those days. He recalled a gondola ride high over the water, a Wild West town, and an arcade where live chickens danced.

The biggest attraction, sometimes referred to as an underwater vaudeville show, was the swimming mermaids. Twice a day visitors boarded a submarine and slowly descended to the lake's bottom. Through large windows, they watched the spectacle, which included a volcano, a swimming pig, a clown, and a giant clamshell that opened to reveal the mermaids. With their shimmering swimsuits and mermaid tails, aqua maids, as they were called, performed a synchronized underwater ballet.

In 1994 Texas State University purchased Spring Lake and the surrounding land with one goal in mind: a transformation. The ecological restoration of the old amusement park took many years, but by 2011 things were finally under way. Crews cleared decrepit structures and debris, like the cables for the skyride, from the land. From the lake, they dug out two submarine theaters as much as fifteen feet underwater. They constructed a wetlands boardwalk and interconnected nature trails. They removed exotic trees and planted native grasses and shrubs. And finally, the refurbished hotel building became the new headquarters for the Meadows Center for Water and the Environment.

The springs below me arose from large fractures, a result of the Balcones fault line, an ancient geological formation that runs through Central Texas. I glided over a sandy stretch known as Cream of Wheat Spring and caught my first glimpse of a red-eared slider, one of the lake's many turtle species. On the bottom seeps gurgled and the sand bubbled up with the current. Unlike springs, the seeps flowed intermittently, more like a slow leak. Due to a drought, the water pushed up to the surface under low pressure that day, but on high-pressure days the springs created a sand geyser. I passed over Salt and Pepper nearby, an area where low-pressure sand boils mixed white gypsum sand and black hummus and looked like the surface of a bubbling pot. Farther down, the lake bottom turned to crumbling rock. The unpredictable terrain, full of nooks and crannies and changing sediments, provided endless possibilities for plants and animals to find a home.

As I glided over the area where the submerged mermaid theater once rested, I asked our guide, a graduate student at the university, the question I always ask on tours: "What is the craziest thing you've ever seen here?"

"Well," he said, and hesitated. "I haven't actually seen one myself, but I've heard that eels gather near the springs. Scuba divers see them at night with flashlights. People say they clump together and climb over the dams."

Back home, I raced to my bookshelf and pulled down a book filled with spectacular underwater photographs of the San Marcos Springs. As I turned the pages, I landed on the image of a shadowlike eel, nearly as long as a young boy, staring back at me.

I knew that eels traveled the rivers and estuaries in Maine, but why I had never heard mention of eels in Central Texas? Questions flooded my mind. Where were the eels in all the waterways? What were they doing in Spring Lake? Did they live there or were they just passing through?

Not long after the summer of whales, my birth family contacted me. I answered the phone, and it was my biological brother. I didn't recognize his name. I sank to the floor and listened to his story. My birth parents had married after high school, and my mother had given birth to two more children, a boy and a girl. My birth parents were still married; they were a family. They had been waiting for me to return.

In some other place—deep within the hearts of strangers—I existed with a different name: Danielle Loren.

Later that night I fell asleep thinking how easily I could have been someone else on some other journey in some other place. My story had shifted again. Set adrift between two worlds, I was unsure to which one I truly belonged.

American eels (*Anguilla rostrata*) are catadromous fish, creatures that travel between freshwater and saltwater environments. Their life cycle is complex, their journey long.

Eels begin life within eggs as small as droplets of rain. They drift near the surface of the Sargasso Sea, an area of the Atlantic Ocean where four currents collide and form a gyre. When the temperatures are right, the eggs hatch and the leaflike larvae, less than an inch long, ride the currents toward land. This may take an entire year. The majority of the larvae end up along the East Coast, but some find themselves on the shores of the Gulf of Mexico. Holes still exist in this part of the story. The how and why of the Gulf Coast larvae remains a mystery.

Over the course of their journey, eels change skins many times. Onshore the larvae transform into glass eels—transparent, snakelike, and several inches long, like rice noodles. From there they begin the journey upstream, where they turn a muddy brown. Less than six inches long, they are known as elvers. They continue to grow, and their skin brightens to a shade of murky yellow. Yellow eels settle into streams or lakes or ponds. For eels, this is the longest life stage.

Male yellow eels remain closer to the sea, while females travel far inland. They feed on small fish, frogs, worms, and insect larvae. Males can grow to be two feet and females over four feet in length. As many as twenty years later the eels undergo another metamorphosis and transform into sexually mature silver eels. They embark on the last phase of their migration, returning to the sea, where they will spawn and die. Throughout the many phases of their lives, eels travel thousands of miles and pass through difficult water-filled terrain.

Although eels' exact location during different life stages has continued to stymie scientists, they believe that eels navigate using various strategies, including all of their senses. Lunar and magnetic cues, for example, come into play along with changes in temperature and even smell. Smells that swirl through the air—the smell of the estuary, of the river, of the springs—may guide eels home and back again.

Historically, big numbers of eels show up in other states along the East Coast, but recently the numbers have declined. One of the reasons is that people have grown an appetite for eel. Glass eels are an Asian delicacy, and eel, also known as unagi, is consumed worldwide in sushi. For fishermen, a pound of eel translates into a big payoff. Eels also face a growing number of obstacles, like hydroelectric dams, along their journey. Because of the declining population in eastern states like Maine, American eels have recently gained more attention.

American eels in Texas have not received as much attention as other karst creatures like bats and salamanders because they are not endemic and their population has always been small. Or perhaps eels never entered our minds because of one unusual possibility: they passed through unseen.

Dean Hendrickson, curator of ichthyology for the University of Texas Biodiversity Collections, started keeping an eye on eels in the Austin area. No one noticed eels near Barton Springs or in Lady Bird Lake until about five years ago. Hendrickson wondered why—had the eels always been there, or had something changed?

In 2017 Hendrickson and Texas Parks and Wildlife biologists collaborated and launched a research project. They hoped to address several key questions: When and how often do eels arrive in Texas, and, once here, are they successful? Do they live long, healthy lives and make it back to the Sargasso Sea to spawn?

In order to answer those questions, the research team needed more information. They asked the public to be on the lookout for eels throughout the state. They asked citizens, naturalists and anglers and divers, to take photos of eels, document locations where they were seen, and, if appropriate, send samples. The data would be used to understand and protect the eels that live, often unseen, in Texas waterways.

I always planned to settle near the ocean in Maine. I spent my childhood summers there with my mother and grandmother, learning about our family roots and exploring the seashore along Union River Bay. That was where I felt most at home.

In the fall my family returned to our home in Virginia near the banks of the Potomac River, but as soon as school ended we followed the familiar route back to Maine. I could hardly wait to set foot on the rocky beaches and peek beneath the seaweed. We lived our lives that way for as long as I could remember, back and forth between salt water and fresh water.

After high school I left Virginia and attended college in Lewiston, Maine, slightly inland near the Androscoggin River. Later I taught high school biology in Camden, a picturesque town along the Maine coast where the briny scent of seaweed drifted through the windows. I married my husband in that same town by the sea.

Then the story changed, as stories sometimes do when two worlds touch. Not long after we married, my husband and I headed to the Texas coast for a yearlong fellowship in Houston. More than twenty years later we still live in Texas, but closer to Austin now in a town where the Comal and Guadalupe Rivers merge. Although I longed to put down roots, I resisted. Longing to stay and find a home, longing to leave and return to the sea—I floated between worlds, neither here nor there.

Instead of putting down roots, I spread outward, like shoots or rootlets or rhizomes, creating a family that grew to include three sons. When my first son was born, I distanced myself from my birth family and dove into protective mode with the instincts of a new mother. I wanted my son to know my adoptive parents, my mother and father, as his family, without a doubt. I wanted my son's feet, and later his brothers' feet, firmly planted in one place. At the time that felt like the right thing to do, but in so doing I created a story full of holes.

One of the holes in the story of the American eel in Texas was this: no one had ever seen a glass eel. On the East Coast, millions of glass eels arrived along the shores like clockwork in late winter and early spring. That didn't appear to be the case along the Texas coast.

According to Hendrickson's data, yellow eels were the only living eels documented in Texas and had been found in small numbers in every river in the state. So somewhere, somehow glass eels and elvers had been making the journey upstream from coastal estuaries and tributaries. The only trace of their existence, however, was a dead silver eel that washed ashore on Padre Island and three long-dead elver specimens housed in a museum. After reading research papers and anything I could get my hands on, I couldn't stop thinking, *Where were they? How did they get here, all the way to Central Texas?*

One day I stumbled on an article by a man who encountered American eels in caves in Florida. Then I uncovered article about subterranean eels in Australia. The more I investigated, the more evidence I found of eels passing through subterranean ecosystems in other parts of the world. Could the existence of subterranean eels be a possibility in Texas?

Certain I wasn't the first to unearth the idea, I posed my question to Hendrickson. His response was quick and enthusiastic: "It seems quite plausible to me that eels could get to Barton Springs by swimming up Onion Creek . . . and then drop down into natural recharge features [holes and cracks] into the aquifer and find their way to Barton Springs underground."

Although eels have not been found in Texas caves, Hendrickson mentioned photographs taken by cave divers that documented the presence of rare American eels inside coastal caves in Mexico. Like a subterranean labyrinth, the water-filled caves and tunnels led to cenotes, deepwater sinkholes, far inland. Just like Texas springs, cenotes revealed something unusual: eels.

It seemed likely then that American eels living in Spring Lake passed between worlds—saltwater and freshwater, the surface and the subterranean. That the natural history of eels far surpassed the myth of mermaids sparked a newfound excitement. Life could happen when we weren't looking, in places we couldn't see, and for reasons we had yet to understand.

Sometimes I chased stories that drifted away or disappeared deep below unseen. And then, from cracked and crumbling places, they reemerged somewhere new. For a nature writer or a biologist or a little girl, the mystery of it all set the stage for an extraordinary tale . . . or perhaps it turned out to be an everyday sort of story, and somehow that made it all the more magical.

Last summer I turned fifty. I had planned to wake up at our family cabin in Maine, as I had done on every birthday as far back as I could remember. But due to chaotic and unpredictable airline travel, I changed plans several times. Finally I found a nonstop flight from Austin to Boston and rented a car for the last leg of the journey.

With Boston in the rearview mirror, I maneuvered into the winding stream of cars headed north for the holiday weekend. My youngest son set up shop in the back seat, pulling out his Nintendo Switch and settling in for the long journey ahead. The rest of the family would join us in a few days.

Soon I was faced with a decision: take the highway or the coastal route, notoriously slow during tourist season. I would normally opt for speed, but something pulled me in a different direction that day; perhaps like the eels, it was the smell of salt water.

Following the coastal route was like chasing memories. Each exit represented a significant event or time period, like the stages of a life cycle. There was the exit where we visited friends with my grandmother every summer; the exit where my parents pulled off to let me wade through the waves; the exit with the seaside trail where my husband proposed; the exit where I headed to the salt marsh with my notebook; the exit that led to the cove where tiny lobsters hid beneath rocks; the exit where I had my first teaching job and where I got married by the sea; and the exit where my mom and I took my children to visit the storybook garden. I pointed out each one to my son as we passed through.

Seven hours later, we pulled into the gravel driveway. In the past my parents would have greeted us, waving from the deck with the bay sparkling behind them. Instead an unsettling stillness greeted us. Then, as startling as the exhale of a whale, my son broke the silence: He threw open the car door, inhaled deeply, and announced, "We're here . . . finally."

As my parents settled into the shallow cracks of my heart, and as my sons began to leave home on their own journeys, a familiar restlessness rippled through my body. A chill, a hint of dampness, and the smell of saltwater floated through the air, triggering change and releasing me from the paper-thin layer of a bedraggled skin.

Being set adrift into the unknown, however unsettling, had always been a secret gift, a chance to chase stories anywhere and everywhere, down into cracks and crevices and holes and then back up again—wherever the restless currents carried me.

CHASING CAVES

"Ready?"

Before I have a chance to answer, Rich Zarria, an expert caver, slings his daypack onto his back and takes off to scour my family's thirty-acre property in Blanco. I try to keep up. We scramble down the steep hillside into the valley, duck under low-lying juniper limbs, and zip up and around the sword-shaped leaves of sotol plants. It feels something like running a cross-country race through an obstacle course only Rich can see.

My family and I have been searching for caves on our property for several years. I learned what to look for by reading books and scientific articles, talking with cavers and scientists, and visiting known caves. We looked for disturbed areas and depressions, unnatural rock jumbles, pieces of trash or old tires sticking up above the ground, sunken areas beneath large tree roots, openings with cool air escaping. Still, after four years, we've come up empty. With my book coming to a close, the time has come to make one last push to locate the caves, but I needed help.

I started by reaching out to the neighbor who, years ago, planted the idea in my head: an older gentleman, whom I met briefly and, by chance, said, "Have you found the caves yet?" In the beginning, asking for the exact location had felt like a cop-out and so, determined to find the caves myself, the search became a family adventure, a way to get to know the land that would become our new home.

After we tracked down the reclusive neighbor, he admitted he hadn't been on the land in years but described an area near the northeast hill: a dangerous drop-off dotted with holes of various sizes, limestone overhangs, and scattered boulders. I knew that slope well and agreed that if the caves existed, that would be the place. Unfortunately dirt and debris had filled the holes, a result of long-term erosion. There was no way to see beyond, to tell where the holes might lead. That, I realized, had been my struggle all along.

During conversations with cavers and scientists over the past few months, one name always popped up: Rich Zarria. He had access to a tool I did not, LiDAR (light detection and ranging) technology. Like radar, which uses radio waves, and sonar, which uses sound waves, LiDAR uses light waves to detect changes in topography. A laser beam sends out a pulse, and the amount of time it takes to reflect back to the lens and sensors is measured and translated into depth information. The beams can be sent through forests, dirt and debris, and other surface features up to two feet belowground.

About ten years ago scientists started using LiDAR systems to pinpoint potential cave-filled areas. In addition to creating reliable data in a rapid manner, the systems themselves can be attached to a variety of vehicles, including airplanes, ATVs, and drones. LiDAR can also be used in conjunction with GPS systems, the perfect combination for detailed 3-D mapmaking.

Zarria, it turns out, had access to online aerial data for the Blanco land. He agreed to help me and contacted me after he gathered the data. One hundred thirty-three anomalies showed up, he reported, but upon further analysis he narrowed the list to the thirty most promising sites. We planned to meet and search the land together. As the date approached, my excitement bubbled to the surface again: thirty seemed like an overabundance of possibility.

Halfway down the far side of the valley, we pause while Zarria pulls out his phone and glances at tiny red pins scattered across the map. We take off in a new direction, toward the dry creek bed. Zarria talks as fast as he moves, like a jackrabbit zigzagging through the brush. A native plant specialist, he points out plants as we pass through them and over them and brush up against them. He shares scientific names as easily as common ones: fragrant mimosa (*Mimosa borealis*), mountain mulberry tree (*Morus microphylla*), Texas madrone (*Arbutus xalapensis*), and devil's shoestring (*Nolina lindheimeriana*), a woody shrub with cream-colored flowers at home on crumbling slopes.

When I catch my breath, I ask Zarria how he became a caver. After his divorce he found himself in a bad space, he explained. One day he went on a hike in search of white avens (*Geum canadense*), a flower he had heard grew in the sinkhole near Hideout Cave in Austin. Although the low-growing groundcover with white flowers, similar to a blackberry bush, is found in other habitats across North America, it is known to thrive in the cool, humid air that escapes caves.

Near the cave Zarria bumped into an old friend, a caver. He convinced Zarria, who was admittedly timid about tight spaces, to join him at a meeting later that night. The Underground Texas Grotto, founded in 1951, meets every month to socialize, share stories of caving expeditions, and plan future trips and training sessions. They welcome and support both beginners and hard-core cavers.

After that night Zarria was hooked, so much so that he began traveling all over the world exploring and discovering hidden caves. The man who had feared heights and tight spaces took to climbing and rappelling up and down sinkholes and cave entrances and squeezing in and out of dark, narrow tunnels, sometimes backward. He quickly made a name for himself, his expeditions attracting the attention of *National Geographic*.

At that time in his life, Zarria needed something to grab hold of, something to guide him through the darkness of his divorce. He needed to keep moving forward, and for him that meant moving at lightning speed through places unknown. Caving became a way to fill that painful void in his life. My own passion for caves and karst ecosystems grew from a dark place as well, a place of sudden loss and change, so I understood that need deeply.

We round the bend at the base of the hill, close to the edge of the property. Until now the stops have been frequent and quick: a spot where a tree had been removed, a sand-filled depression, a swallet or water-carved hole along the creek bank. No caves.

We make our way across a field of knee-high grasses and head toward a cluster of cedar elm trees like an island in the middle of a meadow. Pin number thirty marks a flat, hidden area tucked away beneath the trees—unremarkable really, lacking the allure of a rocky slope or a water-filled depression. Maybe that is why I never looked there, never even considered it. Sweat trickles down my skin. My heart races as our pace slows, as if we are both suddenly aware that this is it, the last possibility.

Zarria pushes through the branches and crouches near a pile of crumbling limestone. The tight space doesn't allow for two bodies, so I wait just beyond. I hold my breath. He clears layers of dead leaves with his hands. He lifts a large rock. I inhale, a short, quick breath. He turns and shakes his head.

The depression is not a cave after all. Zarria steps away, and I take his place on the ground. Although it is not what I had hoped for, it is something: a shallow hole. A temporary shelter.

Unlike natal dens, shallow holes are used by animals like foxes or armadillos to avoid extreme weather or predators, the way smaller beings might use a crack or a crevice. Non-diggers like tarantulas or snakes, which cannot create their own shelters, also move in from time to time, making use of shared subterranean spaces.

Time and again, animals return to these holes and tuck themselves into the landscape. The holes are surprisingly small, just big
enough for a single body to squeeze into and just small enough to
keep the bad things at bay, if only for a moment. In the animal
world, maps of home, including cracks and crevices and holes, are
essential to survival. Committed to memory, these places offer a
safe place to escape. That is how animals navigate rocky terrain—
with a deep understanding of life's cycles, of when to shelter and
when to emerge.

During my own search, the karst places I visited and came to
love—the immense networks of voids and deep depressions and
the shallow cracks near the surface—dot the map of my memory.
They are the places I will return to when I am in need, each one
a temporary shelter.

ACKNOWLEDGMENTS

Not long after finishing this book, I came across a few words that captured the wisdom of how these essays came to be: "The best thing for being sad is to learn something," from *The Book of Merlyn*, by T. H. White.

I am deeply grateful for all of the teachers who have helped me learn something along the way. There have been many, each one unique and unforgettable: Mrs. Taylor who, after recess, let me bring bugs into the classroom and set up my first writing space; Sharon Kinsman, who reminded me that science needs good writers; Coleen O'Connell, who showed me the power of place and of connection—circles and cycles and webs; Sue Eisenfeld, who shared her passion for nature writing and led me through the muck of my first essays and my thesis; Jamie Zvirzdin, who encouraged my worship of sentence structure and my devotion to the em dash; and Vera Dyson, who demonstrated daily that strength and bravery can be found in the quiet and the beautiful.

To all of the people I met, talked to, listened to, emailed, read about, or watched on YouTube while I was on my karst journey, you have been an integral part of this book. Your passion for the Texas Hill Country and its future and your dedication to the conservation of wild subterranean places are awe-inspiring. I look forward to learning more.

To my wild and precious writing group, Laura Gilkey, Heidi Lasher, Anja Semanco, and Elizabeth Domenech, you are all amazingly intelligent, brave, and beautiful women. For two years you have read more about caves and karst than you could have ever dreamt possible. I have learned so much about writing and about life during our time together. Thank you for hanging in there with me.

Thank you to a place that wasn't mentioned in the book but holds a spot deep in my heart: Roughhouse Brewing in San Marcos, where good conversations happened and where life and essays were sorted through. Sitting at a picnic table, Bryant and I mapped our future or at least gave it a shot. I was reminded time and again that there is always time for good music, and a cave-aged beer shared with loved ones never hurts either.

Thank you to Trinity University Press for giving me the opportunity to share my writing.

Thank you to all of my extended family who found their inboxes overflowing and made the time to read my early drafts: Melissa McDivitt, William Frazier, and Diane Forsyth. I appreciate the life experience, wisdom, laughter, and therapeutic conversation you bring to my life.

I am deeply grateful for my very first teachers—my parents, Marigan and Michael Roath, who took me to gorgeous places, filled my life with books, and then pushed me out the door. Even in your absence, your love leads me home.

Thank you to my children: Jackson Kyle, Keenan Matthew, and Ryland James. You have taught me more about how to be a human being than you can imagine. I hope you continue to ignite your own curiosity and live your lives as an experiment, always willing to wander and see life from a different perspective. And, of course, may we always find new ways to weird it out together.

For my husband, Bryant, I am most grateful. From the early sea star mishaps to looping lizards and cloud gazing, to watching our children leave home, you have been my partner on the biggest journey. I can't imagine stumbling through life with anyone else. You have taught me the joy of enduring love and the beauty of carving out a life together. It really is a team sport, especially when shift happens. (Nope, still not a good title for the book, but I appreciate your persistence.) Thank you for listening to and reading and living all of these subterranean stories. It certainly was a good thing you had on your hard hat that day. Without a doubt, it was a foreshadowing. And as Ryland and the Imagine Dragons (sort of) would say:

I will follow you way down
wherever you may go,
I will follow you way down into the deepest holes.

Laurie Roath Frazier is a naturalist, educator, and science writer. She lives in the Texas Hill Country.

Printed in the USA
CPSIA information can be obtained
at www.ICGtesting.com
JSHW020302230724
66773JS00005B/8

9 781595 342881